Dreamweaver CS5: Basic

Instructor's Edition

ACA Edition

Dreamweaver CS5: Basic, ACA Edition

President, Axzo Press:	Jon Winder
Vice President, Product Development:	Charles G. Blum
Vice President, Operations:	Josh Pincus
Director of Publishing Systems Development:	Dan Quackenbush
Writer:	Brandon Heffernan
Copyeditor:	Catherine Oliver
Keytester:	Cliff Coryea

Trademarks

ILT Series is a trademark of Axzo Press.

Some of the product names and company names used in this book have been used for identification purposes only and may be trademarks or registered trademarks of their respective manufacturers and sellers.

Disclaimers

We reserve the right to revise this publication and make changes from time to time in its content without notice.

The Adobe Approved Certification Courseware logo is either a registered trademark or trademark of Adobe Systems Incorporated in the United States and/or other countries. The Adobe Approved Certification Courseware logo is a proprietary trademark of Adobe. All rights reserved.

The ILT Series is independent from ProCert Labs, LLC and Adobe Systems Incorporated, and are not affiliated with ProCert Labs and Adobe in any manner. This publication may assist students to prepare for an Adobe Certified Expert exam, however, neither ProCert Labs nor Adobe warrant that use of this material will ensure success in connection with any exam.

ISBN 10: 1-4260-2088-0
ISBN 13: 978-1-4260-2088-9

Printed in the United States of America

2 3 4 5 6 7 8 9 10 GL 13 12 11

Contents

Introduction   **iii**

Topic A: About the manual...iv
Topic B: Setting student expectations ix
Topic C: Classroom setup..xiii
Topic D: Support...xvi

Getting started   **1-1**

Topic A: Internet basics 1-2
Topic B: Project management basics...1-5
Topic C: The Dreamweaver CS5 interface.......................................1-13
Topic D: Basic editing 1-27
Unit summary: Getting started 1-33

Web sites and pages   **2-1**

Topic A: Planning tools and design principles 2-2
Topic B: Defining and building a site..2-8
Topic C: Working with code 2-22
Unit summary: Web sites and pages 2-34

Structure and style   **3-1**

Topic A: Structure...3-2
Topic B: Cascading Style Sheets..3-11
Unit summary: Structure and style..3-28

Tables   **4-1**

Topic A: Creating tables 4-2
Topic B: Table structure and formatting..4-10
Unit summary: Tables 4-19

Links   **5-1**

Topic A: Creating links...5-2
Topic B: Applying link styles..5-13
Unit summary: Links...5-16

Image formats and attributes   **6-1**

Topic A: Working with images..6-2
Unit summary: Image formats and attributes...................................6-11

Publishing   **7-1**

Topic A: Site checks and publishing..7-2
Unit summary: Publishing...7-16

Course summary   **S-1**

Topic A: Course summary...S-2
Topic B: Continued learning after class S-4

Glossary   **G-1**

Index   **I-1**

Introduction

After reading this introduction, you'll know how to:

A Use ILT Series manuals in general.

B Use prerequisites, a target student description, course objectives, and a skills inventory to set student expectations properly for the course.

C Set up a classroom to teach this course.

D Get support for setting up and teaching this course.

Topic A: About the manual

ILT Series philosophy

Our goal is to make you, the instructor, as successful as possible. To that end, our manuals facilitate students' learning by providing structured interaction with the software itself. While we provide text to help you explain difficult concepts, the hands-on activities are the focus of our courses. Leading the students through these activities will teach the skills and concepts effectively.

We believe strongly in the instructor-led class. For many students, having a thinking, feeling instructor in front of them is always the most comfortable way to learn. Because the students' focus should be on you, our manuals are designed and written to facilitate your interaction with the students and not to call attention to manuals themselves.

We believe in the basic approach of setting expectations, then teaching, and providing summary and review afterwards. For this reason, lessons begin with objectives and end with summaries. We also provide overall course objectives and a course summary to provide both an introduction to and closure on the entire course.

Our goal is your success. We encourage your feedback in helping us to improve our manuals continually to meet your needs.

Manual components

The manuals contain these major components:

- Table of contents
- Introduction
- Units
- Course summary
- Glossary
- Index

Each element is described below.

Table of contents

The table of contents acts as a learning roadmap for you and the students.

Introduction

The introduction contains information about our training philosophy and our manual components, features, and conventions. It contains target student, prerequisite, objective, and setup information for the specific course. Finally, the introduction contains support information.

Units

Units are the largest structural component of the actual course content. A unit begins with a title page that lists objectives for each major subdivision, or topic, within the unit. Within each topic, conceptual and explanatory information alternates with hands-on activities. Units conclude with a summary comprising one paragraph for each topic, and an independent practice activity that gives students an opportunity to practice the skills they've learned.

The conceptual information takes the form of text paragraphs, exhibits, lists, and tables. The activities are structured in two columns, one telling students what to do, the other providing explanations, descriptions, and graphics. Throughout a unit, instructor notes are found in the left margin.

Course summary

This section provides a text summary of the entire course. It's useful for providing closure at the end of the course. The course summary also indicates the next course in this series, if there is one, and lists additional resources students might find useful as they continue to learn about the software.

Glossary

The glossary provides definitions for all of the key terms used in this course.

Index

The index at the end of this manual makes it easy for you and your students to find information about a particular software component, feature, or concept.

Manual conventions

We've tried to keep the number of elements and the types of formatting to a minimum in the manuals. We think this approach aids in clarity and makes the manuals more elegant looking. But there are some conventions and icons you should know about.

Instructor note/icon

Item	Description
Italic text	In conceptual text, indicates a new term or feature.
Bold text	In unit summaries, indicates a key term or concept. In an independent practice activity, indicates an explicit item that you select, choose, or type.
`Code font`	Indicates code or syntax.
`Longer strings of ▶ code will look ▶ like this.`	In the hands-on activities, any code that's too long to fit on a single line is divided into segments by one or more continuation characters (▶). This code should be entered as a continuous string of text.
	In the left margin, provide tips, hints, and warnings for the instructor.
Select **bold item**	In the left column of hands-on activities, bold sans-serif text indicates an explicit item that you select, choose, or type.
Keycaps like (↵ ENTER)	Indicate a key on the keyboard you must press.
⚠ Warning icon.	Warnings prepare instructors for potential classroom management problems.
✔ Tip icon.	Tips give extra information the instructor can share with students.
Setup icon.	Setup notes provide a realistic business context for instructors to share with students, or indicate additional setup steps required for the current activity.
Projector icon.	Projector notes indicate that there is a PowerPoint slide for the adjacent content.

Instructor notes.

Hands-on activities

The hands-on activities are the most important parts of our manuals. They're divided into two primary columns. The "Here's how" column gives short directions to the students. The "Here's why" column provides explanations, graphics, and clarifications. To the left, instructor notes provide tips, warnings, setups, and other information for the instructor only. Here's a sample:

Do it!

A-1: Creating a commission formula

Here's how	Here's why
1 Open Sales	This is an oversimplified sales compensation worksheet. It shows sales totals, commissions, and incentives for five sales reps.
2 Observe the contents of cell F4	F4 ▼ = =E4*C_Rate The commission rate formulas use the name "C_Rate" instead of a value for the commission rate.

Take the time to make sure your students understand this worksheet. We'll be here a while.

For these activities, we've provided a collection of data files designed to help students learn each skill in a real-world business context. As students work through the activities, they'll modify and update these files. Of course, students might make a mistake and, therefore, want to re-key the activity starting from scratch. To make it easy to start over, students rename each data file at the end of the first activity in which the file is modified. Our convention for renaming files is to add the word "My" to the beginning of the file name. In the above activity, for example, students are using a file called "Sales" for the first time. At the end of this activity, they save the file as "My sales," thus leaving the "Sales" file unchanged. If students make mistakes, they can start over using the original "Sales" file.

In some activities, however, it might not be practical to rename the data file. Such exceptions are indicated with an instructor note. If students want to retry one of these activities, you need to provide a fresh copy of the original data file.

PowerPoint presentations

Each unit in this course has an accompanying PowerPoint presentation. These slide shows are designed to support your classroom instruction while providing students with a visual focus. Each presentation begins with a list of unit objectives and ends with a unit summary slide. We strongly recommend that you run these presentations from the instructor's station as you teach this course. A copy of PowerPoint Viewer is included, so it is not necessary to have PowerPoint installed on your computer.

The ILT Series PowerPoint add-in

The CD also contains a PowerPoint add-in that enables you to create slide notes for the class.

To load the PowerPoint add-in:

1 Copy the Course_ILT.ppa file to a convenient location on your hard drive.

2 Start PowerPoint.

3 Choose Tools, Macro, Security to open the Security dialog box. On the Security Level tab, select Medium (if necessary), and then click OK.

4 Choose Tools, Add-Ins to open the Add-Ins dialog box. Then, click Add New.

5 Browse to and double-click the Course_ILT.ppa file, and then click OK. A message box will appear, warning you that macros can contain viruses.

6 Click Enable Macros. The Course_ILT add-in should now appear in the Available Add-Ins list (in the Add-Ins dialog box). The "x" in front of Course_ILT indicates that the add-in is loaded.

7 Click Close to close the Add-Ins dialog box.

After you complete this procedure, a new toolbar will be available at the top of the PowerPoint window. This toolbar contains a single button labeled "Create SlideNotes." Click this button to generate slide-notes files in both text (.txt) and Excel (.xls) format. By default, these files will be saved to the folder that contains the presentation. If the PowerPoint file is on a CD-ROM or in some other location to which the slide-notes files cannot be saved, you will be prompted to save the presentation to your hard drive and try again.

Topic B: Setting student expectations

Properly setting students' expectations is essential to your success. This topic will help you do that by providing:

- Prerequisites for this course
- A description of the target student
- A list of the objectives for the course
- A skills assessment for the course

Course prerequisites

Students taking this course should be familiar with personal computers and the use of a keyboard and a mouse. Furthermore, this course assumes that students have completed the following courses or have equivalent experience:

- *Windows 7: Basic, Windows Vista: Basic, or Windows XP: Basic*

Target student

This course will benefit students who want to learn how to use Dreamweaver CS5 to create and modify Web sites. Students will learn how to plan, define, and create a Web site; add pages and content; format text; create and apply CSS styles; create links and tables; manage images and other files; and publish a site. Students taking this course should be comfortable using a PC and have experience with Microsoft Windows 7, Vista, or XP. Students should have little or no experience with Dreamweaver.

Adobe ACA certification

This course is designed to help your students pass the Adobe Certified Associate (ACA) exam for Dreamweaver CS5. For complete certification training, students should complete this course and *Dreamweaver CS5: Advanced, ACA Edition.*

Course objectives

You should share these overall course objectives with your students at the beginning of the day. This approach will give them an idea about what to expect, and it will help you identify students who might be misplaced. Students are considered misplaced when they lack the prerequisite knowledge or when they already know most of the subject matter to be covered.

Note: In addition to the general objectives listed below, specific ACA exam objectives are listed at the beginning of each topic (where applicable) and are highlighted by instructor notes throughout each unit. For a complete mapping of ACA objectives to ILT Series content, see Appendix A.

After completing this course, students will know how to:

- Discuss basic Internet and HTML concepts; discuss basic project management principles, effective communications management, and Web site planning; identify the components of the Dreamweaver CS5 workspace; create a custom workspace; edit and format text; insert images; and preview pages in a browser.

- Employ planning tools such as flowcharts, storyboards, and wireframes; identify and apply basic principles of design; define a Web site; work with the Files panel and the Assets panel; create a Web page; import text from external files; set basic page properties; identify basic HTML tags; switch between document views; work with code and the code tools; insert special characters; and use the Find and Replace dialog box to update content and code.

- Define a basic page structure; create and modify lists; create CSS style sheets; apply styles to text; and create class styles.

- Create tables and nested tables; write effective table summaries; format rows and cells; merge cells; add rows and columns; set fixed and variable widths for tables and columns; and change cell borders and padding.

- Create links to other pages and resources; create named anchors and link to them; create e-mail links; create image maps; and apply CSS styles to link states.

- Choose appropriate image formats; write effective alternate text; modify image properties; and insert and modify background images.

- Recognize copyright issues; check file size and download times; check for spelling errors; check for broken links and orphaned files; cloak files; connect to a remote server; and upload and update a site.

Skills inventory

Use the following form to gauge students' skill levels entering the class (students have copies in the introductions of their student manuals). For each skill listed, have students rate their familiarity from 1 to 5, with five being the most familiar. Emphasize that this isn't a test. Rather, it's intended to provide students with an idea of where they're starting from at the beginning of class. If a student is wholly unfamiliar with all the skills, he or she might not be ready for the class. A student who seems to understand all of the skills, on the other hand, might need to move on to the next course in the series.

Skill	1	2	3	4	5
Discussing basic Internet, HTML, and XHTML concepts					
Discussing basic principles of project management, communications management, and Web site planning					
Identifying components of the Dreamweaver CS5 workspace					
Creating a custom workspace					
Using the Workspace Switcher					
Inserting, editing, and formatting text					
Inserting images					
Previewing pages in a browser					
Applying planning tools such as flowcharts, storyboards, and wireframes					
Discussing basic design principles					
Defining a local site					
Working with the Files panel and the Assets panel					
Creating and titling Web pages					
Importing text					
Setting page properties					
Identifying basic HTML tags					
Switching between document views					
Working with code and the code tools					
Inserting special characters and nonbreaking spaces					
Using Find and Replace to update content or code					
Defining a page structure					

Skill	1	2	3	4	5
Creating and modifying lists					
Creating and attaching external style sheets					
Defining element styles with CSS					
Creating and applying class styles					
Creating and modifying tables					
Writing effective table summaries					
Creating nested tables					
Formatting table cells, rows, and columns					
Applying fixed and variable table widths					
Creating links to other pages and resources					
Creating named anchors and linking to them					
Creating e-mail links					
Creating image maps					
Applying CSS styles to link states					
Choosing appropriate image formats					
Writing effective alternate text					
Modifying image properties					
Inserting and modifying background images					
Recognizing copyright issues					
Checking file size and download times					
Checking for spelling errors					
Fixing broken links					
Locating orphaned files					
Cloaking files and folders					
Connecting to a remote server					
Uploading and updating a site					

Topic C: Classroom setup

All our courses assume that each student has a personal computer to use during the class. Our hands-on approach to learning requires that they do. This topic gives information on how to set up the classroom to teach this course.

Hardware requirements

Each student's personal computer should have:

- A keyboard and a mouse
- Intel® Pentium® 4 or equivalent processor
- 512 MB RAM
- 1 GB of hard disk space for Dreamweaver CS5 installation; additional space needed for operating system and Office installation
- A DVD-ROM drive for installation
- A monitor set to a minimum resolution of 1280 × 960 and 24-bit color or better (Users of LCD or widescreen displays should choose the monitor's native resolution, if possible.)

Software requirements

You need the following software:

- Windows 7, Windows Vista, or Windows XP with Service Pack 3
- Dreamweaver CS5
- Microsoft Outlook, Thunderbird, or another e-mail client (required to complete Activity A-3 in the "Links" unit)
- Microsoft Word 2000 or later version (required to complete Activity B-3 in the "Web sites and pages" unit)

Network requirements

The following network components and connectivity are also required for this course:

- Internet access, for the following purposes:
  - Downloading the latest critical updates and service packs
  - Downloading the Student Data files from www.axzopress.com (if necessary)
  - Visiting and discussing designs on the Web, and completing Activity A-3 in the "Links" unit

Classroom setup instructions

Before you teach this course, you will need to perform the following steps to set up each student computer.

1   Install Windows 7 on an NTFS partition according to the software publisher's instructions. After installation is complete, if the student machines have Internet access, use Windows Update to install any critical updates and Service Packs.

> **Note:** You can also use Windows Vista or Windows XP with Service Pack 3, but the screen shots in this course were taken in Windows 7, so students' screens might look somewhat different.

2   With flat-panel displays, we recommend using the panel's native resolution for best results. Color depth/quality should be set to High (24 bit) or higher.

3   Verify that Internet Explorer is the default Web browser.

   a   Click Start and choose All Programs, Internet Explorer.

   b   Configure Internet Explorer as prompted. Do not turn on Suggested Sites, and use express settings.

   c   Choose Tools, Internet Options.

   d   On the Programs tab, click Make default, and click OK.

   e   Close Internet Explorer.

4   Install Dreamweaver CS5 according to the software manufacturer's instructions.

5   Install Microsoft Office 2000, XP, 2003, or 2007 according to the software manufacturer's instructions. Accept all defaults during installation. (This step is required to complete Activity B-2 in the "Web sites and pages" unit.)

6   For each student, create an e-mail account in the installed e-mail client. (Students don't actually send or receive messages in this course, so a fully functional e-mail account isn't needed. Without an e-mail client, students can't complete Activity A-3 in the "Links" unit.)

7   Display file extensions:

   a   Open Windows Explorer.

   b   (In Windows 7) Choose Organize, Folder and search options; then click the View tab.

   c   Clear the check box for "Hide extensions for known file types." Click OK.

   d   Close Windows Explorer.

8 If you have the data disc that came with this manual, locate the Student Data folder on it and copy it to the desktop of each student computer.

If you don't have the data disc, you can download the Student Data files for the course:

a Connect to www.axzopress.com.

b Under Downloads, click Instructor-Led Training.

c Browse the subject categories to locate your course. Then click the course title to display a list of available downloads. (You can also access these downloads through our Catalog listings.)

d Click the link(s) for downloading the Student Data files. You can download the files directly to student machines or to a central location on your own network.

e Create a folder named Student Data on the desktop of each student computer.

f Double-click the downloaded zip file(s) and drag the contents into the Student Data folder.

CertBlaster exam preparation for ACA certification

CertBlaster pre- and post-assessment software is available for this course. To download and install this free software, students should complete the following steps:

1 Go to www.axzopress.com.

2 Under Downloads, click CertBlaster.

3 Click the link for Dreamweaver CS5.

4 Save the .EXE file to a folder on your hard drive. (**Note:** If you skip this step, the CertBlaster software will not install correctly.)

5 Click Start and choose Run.

6 Click Browse and navigate to the folder that contains the .EXE file.

7 Select the .EXE file and click Open.

8 Click OK and follow the on-screen instructions. When prompted for the password, enter **c_dwcs5**.

Topic D: Support

Your success is our primary concern. If you need help setting up this class or teaching a particular unit, topic, or activity, please don't hesitate to get in touch with us.

Contacting us

Please contact us through our Web site, www.axzopress.com. You will need to provide the name of the course, and be as specific as possible about the kind of help you need.

Instructor's tools

Our Web site provides several instructor's tools for each course, including course outlines and answers to frequently asked questions. To download these files, go to www.axzopress.com. Then, under Downloads, click Instructor-Led Training and browse our subject categories.

Unit 1

Getting started

Unit time: 75 minutes

Complete this unit, and you'll know how to:

A Discuss basic Internet, HTML, and XHTML concepts.

B Discuss basic project management principles, effective communications management, and Web site planning concepts.

C Identify components of the Dreamweaver CS5 workspace, and create a custom workspace.

D Insert and edit text, insert images and provide a text alternative, and preview a page in a browser.

Topic A: Internet basics

Explanation

Before you start using Dreamweaver CS5 to design and create Web sites, you should first understand the basics of the Internet, the Web, and HTML.

The Internet and the Web

The *Internet* is a vast array of networks that belong to universities, businesses, organizations, governments, and individuals all over the world. The World Wide Web, or simply the *Web*, is one of many services of the Internet. Other Internet services include e-mail, File Transfer Protocol (FTP), and instant messaging.

To view Web pages and other content, you need a Web browser, such as Internet Explorer, Firefox, or Safari. Web content typically includes text, images, and multimedia files. Each page or resource has a unique address known as a *Uniform Resource Locater* (URL).

A *Web site* is a collection of linked pages. The top-level page is commonly called the *home page*. A home page typically provides hyperlinks to navigate to other pages within the site or to external pages. A *hyperlink*—or more commonly, a *link*—is text or an image that, when clicked, takes the user to another page, another location on the current page, another Web site, or a specific file.

HTML

Hypertext Markup Language, or *HTML,* is a standard markup language on the Web. HTML enables you to structure and present your Web site's content. An HTML document is a plain text file that contains HTML code, along with the content for a Web page. Exhibit 1-1 shows an example of a simple HTML document. HTML documents have an .htm or .html file extension.

HTML code encloses your text content and defines the basic structure of a Web page. A Web page can contain links, images, multimedia files, and other elements. When a browser opens a Web page, the text typically loads quickly, while images and embedded media files might take longer.

XHTML

Extensible Hypertext Markup Language, or *XHTML,* is a more efficient and strict version of HTML. For years, browser makers introduced proprietary tags and attributes in an effort to give Web designers more control over the look and feel of their Web pages. Unfortunately, most of these elements and attributes served only to make Web page code bloated, cluttered, and semantically meaningless. Because XHTML doesn't allow proprietary tags or attributes, the result is cleaner, more efficient code that is more evenly supported across different browsers. Dreamweaver CS5 builds Web pages with XHTML code by default.

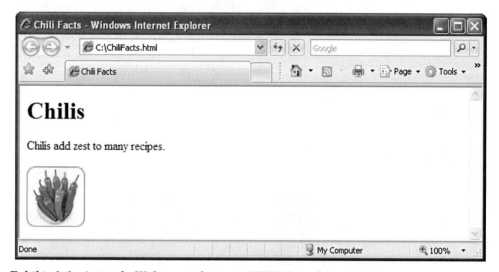

```
<!DOCTYPE html PUBLIC "-//W3C//DTD XHTML 1.0 Transitional//EN" "http://
<html xmlns="http://www.w3.org/1999/xhtml">
<head>
<meta http-equiv="Content-Type" content="text/html; charset=utf-8" />
<title>Chili Facts</title>
</head>

<body>
<h1>Chilis</h1>
<p>Chilis add zest to many recipes. </p>
<img src="chilis.jpg" alt="Chilis" />
</body>
</html>
```

Exhibit 1-1: A simple Web page shown as XHTML code and in a browser

Do it!

A-1: Discussing the Web, HTML, and XHTML

Questions and answers

You might be able to lead off with this activity to determine the knowledge and experience levels of your students.

Ask for student volunteers and facilitate a brief discussion.

1 What's the difference between the Internet and the World Wide Web?

The Internet is a vast network of smaller networks. The networks of universities, businesses, organizations, governments, and individuals all over the world form the Internet. The Web is one of the many services of the Internet.

2 What other Internet services are there?

Answers might vary, but should include FTP (File Transfer Protocol), e-mail, and instant messaging.

3 What's a Web page?

A Web page is an HTML document that's typically viewed in a Web browser. Web pages can contain text, images, and multimedia files.

4 What's a Web site?

A collection of linked Web pages.

5 What's a Web browser?

A software application used to view and interact with Web pages.

6 What's HTML?

HTML is a standard markup language for Web pages. HTML code defines the structure of the document, encloses the text, defines basic formatting, and provides links to resources, such as images, multimedia files, and other Web pages.

7 What's XHTML?

XHTML is a stricter version of HTML that doesn't allow proprietary tags or attributes, resulting in cleaner, more efficient code. By default, Dreamweaver CS5 builds Web pages with XHTML.

Topic B: Project management basics

This topic covers the following Adobe ACA exam objectives for Dreamweaver CS5.

#	Objective
1.1a	Identify information that determines the purpose, audience, and audience needs for a website.
1.2a	Identify criteria for determining whether content is relevant to the website's purpose.
1.2b	Identify criteria for determining whether content is appropriate for the target audience.
1.5a	Demonstrate knowledge of the relationship between end-user requirements and design and development decisions.
1.5b	Identify page elements that are affected by end-user technical factors, such as download speed, screen resolution, operating system, and browser type.
1.6a	Identify items that might appear on a project plan.
1.6b	Identify phases that might appear on a project plan.
1.6c	Identify deliverables that might be produced during the project.
1.6d	Identify common problems and issues in project management.
2.6	Communicate with others (such as peers and clients) about design and content plans.

Project planning

Explanation

Before you begin creating and modifying pages in Dreamweaver, you should have a project plan in place so that your work is focused, efficient, and ultimately effective. Having a project plan in place before you get started will also help you manage unexpected problems that might arise. Before you explore site planning considerations, it's helpful to have a foundation in project management concepts.

Project phases

ACA objective 1.6b

A project is an organized effort to achieve a goal that has a deliverable. A project is a temporary endeavor, with a defined purpose, scope, and end. Project management is an iterative process that involves the following five phases: initiating; planning; executing; monitoring and controlling; and closing. These phases, shown in Exhibit 1-2, require careful planning and monitoring to ensure a successful project.

Collectively, these phases represent the *project lifecycle*. During each project phase, one or more outputs are completed. Outputs must be realistic and measurable; otherwise they have no meaning. Only when outputs are measurable can you determine whether the project is proceeding as planned.

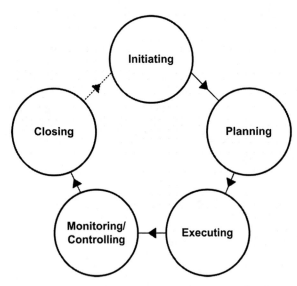

Exhibit 1-2: The five phases of project management

The following table describes each phase of the project lifecycle.

	Phase	Description	Output examples
ACA objective 1.6b	Initiating	You define and authorize the project, name the project manager, and define the project scope, deliverables, duration, and resources.	A project charter
ACA objective 1.6a	Planning	You identify your resource requirements, stakeholders, and the scope of the project. You define the project objectives and requirements, develop the schedule, set the budget, identify risks, assign resources, and plan procurement.	A project management plan
ACA objective 1.6c	Executing	You implement the project management plan, complete the work, and coordinate staff.	Deliverables, such as design mockups, pages ready for accessibility and usability testing, and progress reports
	Monitoring/ Controlling	You monitor performance against the project management plan, identify variances, take corrective action when necessary, and implement approved changes.	Corrective actions, such as changing design and usability elements, correcting errors, and applying client feedback
	Closing	You formalize the acceptance of the project and ensure an orderly end. You gather project information, review the project's time and cost performance, compile lessons learned, and close contracts.	Sign-off from the client or sponsor

ACA objective 1.6d

During the initiating and planning phases, the project needs are identified and the outcomes of the project are defined. These phases require the project manager to perform the following tasks:

- Identify the objectives clearly.
- Identify the project's scope.
- Translate business requirements into functional and technical requirements.
- Estimate time and cost requirements.
- Link activities to performance and deliverables.
- Establish priorities and ground rules.
- Identify risks.
- Negotiate; for example, for funding or resources.

Common problems

ACA objective 1.6d

In discussing reasons for project failures, encourage students to share their experiences.

Sometimes projects don't go as planned. You can avoid some of the common causes of failure by being aware of what has caused previous projects to fail. There are a multitude of reasons that some projects fall short of their objectives, but some reasons are more common than others. A successful project manager anticipates and addresses potential problems while planning the project.

The following factors are typical contributors to project failure:

- **Sponsor not involved** — A sponsor who isn't actively involved in setting the project's strategy and direction can quickly doom a project. Without the support of a sponsor, a project can lose its funding and support from senior management.
- **Poor project planning** — A project plan that's nonexistent, out-of-date, incomplete, or poorly constructed significantly increases the likelihood that a project will fail.
- **Frequent project manager changes** — A project team can't be cohesive without a good leader. Trust and leadership are essential to a project and are typically built over time.
- **Responsibilities not clear** — Sometimes projects use external contractors to accomplish one or more tasks. When the responsibilities of the external service providers and in-house staff are not clearly defined, important tasks often fall through the cracks.
- **Unclear benefits and deliverables** — If the benefits of the project and the way they will be delivered aren't well defined, you probably won't have a satisfactory level of "buy-in" among project participants.
- **Poor or no change control** — If changes in a project are not carefully controlled, the project can quickly get out of hand. A project's scope can expand, or "creep," making it difficult or impossible to deliver on time.
- **Changes in technology** — Changes in technology during a project can cause it to fail if a technology that was planned for is no longer utilized or optimal.
- **Inappropriate or insufficient skills** — If project team members don't have the required knowledge or skill level, deliverables might be late or the project might fail completely.

- **Scope creep** — Scope creep is the addition of project requirements while the project is in process. Scope creep often occurs when project sponsors or business unit managers don't adequately understand their needs and business requirements. It also occurs because new technologies, which aren't part of the project plan, become available and are suddenly added to the project as requirements. Scope creep can also occur when managers outside the original project definition suddenly understand the benefits of a project's deliverables and want their departments added to the project. A good project manager must handle scope creep in a diplomatic and productive manner to keep the project on track.

- **Ineffective project manager** — Poor project managers are either not trained in project management best practices or are a poor fit from a personality point of view. Examples of ineffective project managers include micromanagers and those who ignore problems as they arise.

Project communication

A communications management plan is often needed to ensure the smooth flow of information among the stakeholders involved in a project—including the project sponsor or client, the project manager, the project team, end-users, and sellers—so that they can make informed decisions throughout the project. This plan describes who needs to receive information, what information is needed, when it's needed, and how it should be disseminated.

The first purpose of a communications management plan is to ensure that communication does occur. The best intentions can fall by the wayside if a project manager is faced with requests from all sides. If communications are planned from the outset, the project manager can allocate time to perform this critical function.

A communications management plan must also ensure that communication is done right. A good communication plan determines who needs what information, and when.

Collaborate with a project team using CS Live

ACA objective 2.6

For creative projects, such as Web design and development projects, effective communication often involves review and revision as an ongoing and recursive process. Valuable time can be wasted if fast and efficient communication isn't available. To help make this process more efficient, you can use CS Live, a service available with any Adobe CS5 application.

For example, by using CS Review, a service of CS Live, you can initiate a design review and invite colleagues or clients to provide feedback by using their Web browsers. To use CS Live services, you need to establish a CS Live account. Services are free for a limited time. To begin using CS Live, click the CS Live button at the top of the application window and select an option.

Do it!   **B-1:   Discussing basic project management concepts**

Here's how

Spend time reviewing these concepts with the class as a group.

ACA objective 1.6b

ACA objective 1.6a

ACA objective 1.6d

ACA objective 2.6

1 What's a project?

   An organized effort toward a goal that has a deliverable. It is a temporary endeavor.

2 What are the five phases of a project?

   Initiating, planning, executing, monitoring/controlling, and closing.

3 During the planning phase, a project plan is produced. What items might appear in the project plan?

   The scope of the project and resource requirements—stakeholders, objectives and requirements, schedule, budget, risks, resources, and procurement strategies.

4 Why is planning important to the success of a project?

   Planning helps identify the project scope, the task and resource requirements, and other critical project variables. Without an effective plan, a project is not likely to succeed.

5 What are some common problems that can contribute to a project's failure?

   An uninvolved sponsor, poor planning, frequent management changes, unclear responsibilities, unclear benefits and deliverables, poor or no change control, changes in technology, inappropriate or insufficient skills, scope creep, and poor project managers.

6 What are some ways you can ensure effective communication when working on a Web site project?

   Answers will vary but may include developing a communications plan and using technology such as CS Live, which includes CS Review.

Web project planning

Explanation

When you start a new Web site, it's important to first plan the site project carefully before you begin developing the design and content.

Basic elements of a site project plan

When you plan your Web site's design, consider more than your visual design approach. Other factors, including accessibility, structure, navigation, and consistent rendering in multiple browsers, are equally important.

Also, a critical component of any Web development project is an analysis of the site's purpose and its intended audience. More specifically, keep these factors in mind before you begin development:

ACA objectives 1.2a, 1.2b

- **Audience** — Analyze the interests, age, experiences, background, and expectations of your audience. You'll find that many of your later design choices are based on this analysis.
- **Objective** — Set well-defined objectives for your Web site. An objective should be specific, measurable, and realistic.
- **Content** — The content should clearly convey the purpose of the site and it should be relevant to the intended users. The language, tone, graphics, and level of detail should be based on an analysis of the site's objectives and target audience.
- **Site structure** — Finalize the navigation structure at the beginning of the design process. Changing the site structure later can be costly and time consuming.

Analyzing a site's purpose and audience

ACA objectives 1.1a, 1.2a

It's important to spend some time defining the audience for the site and the goals you want to accomplish with the site. Ask yourself or your team the following general questions as part of a comprehensive (and ongoing) analysis:

ACA objective 1.2b

- What do we (or what does the client) want to achieve with the site?
- How will the site achieve the established goals?
- Whom are we trying to reach, and what are the audience demographics—the education level, age range, gender, or special interests of the target audience?
- What does the intended audience already know about the information that will be presented on the site?
- What values or experiences might members of this audience have in common?
- What are the client's goals?
- In what ways will the audience be transformed or edified by the information presented on the Web site?

ACA objective 1.5a

- How will we keep visitors interested and engaged over the long term?
- What are the specific needs of the site's users, and how will we tailor the design and content to those needs?

ACA objective 1.5b

- Which browsers are predominantly used by the target audience?
- What Internet access speed is typical, on average, for the target audience?

Design considerations

ACA objective 1.5a

You can attract and retain users by designing pages that make it easy for them to find the information they're looking for. You can do this with a blend of colors, graphics, content, and navigational aids. Before you begin actual design and content work, think about how best to structure the site's content and how you want to present information.

When you plan a site's design and structure, keep the following factors in mind:

- **Navigation** — The navigation scheme should reflect the site's structure, and it should be consistent on every page.

- **Fonts** — Choose fonts that provide optimal readability and that suit the target audience. For example, you might use standard fonts, such as Arial and Times New Roman for a corporate site, but a more playful font, such as Comic Sans MS, for a site targeted to kids.

ACA objective 1.5b

- **Page length** — Break information into manageable chunks. A page that contains excessive text and requires a lot of vertical scrolling can be tedious to users.

- **Visual contrast** — Make sure your background color and text color have sufficient contrast so that the text is clear, crisp, and easy to read.

- **Load time** — Use graphics and other potentially "heavy" components conservatively. You can lose visitors if it takes too long for your pages to load.

- **Headings** — Use headings carefully. They should serve as titles or brief descriptors for the content beneath them.

B-2: Discussing basic design considerations

Questions and answers

1 What are some important factors to consider when planning a Web site?

   Answers might include:

   - *Audience*

   - *Objective*

   - *Content*

   - *Site structure*

2 What content factors are important to consider when planning a site?

   Answers may vary. The content should clearly convey the purpose of the site and it should be relevant to the intended users. The language, tone, graphics, and level of detail should be based on an analysis of the site's objectives and target audience.

3 What questions can you ask yourself or your project team to help ensure that content and design choices stay relevant to the site's overall purpose?

   Items might include:

   - *What do we (or what does the client) want to achieve with the site?*

   - *Whom are we trying to reach, and what are the audience demographics—the education level, age range, gender, or special interests of the target audience?*

   - *What does the intended audience already know about the information that will be presented on the site?*

   - *How will we keep visitors interested and engaged over the long term?*

4 You have determined that your site's audience is composed solely of people in a corporation using high-speed access and a standard browser. What design decisions might be affected by this information?

   Answers may vary. If access speeds and browsers are known and consistent, you can be less concerned about the number of images in use and their impact on download time. Also, you don't need to spend time testing the site in multiple browsers and operating systems.

5 Why is it important to choose background colors and text colors carefully?

   If there isn't sufficient contrast between text color and background color, content can be difficult to read and might strain the user's eyes. Also, color plays an important role in the overall design of the site. Good color choices can help enhance the message you're trying to convey.

6 Why is it important to break text into logical, manageable chunks?

   To hold the user's interest. Long sections of text that require vertical scrolling can be tedious to read.

Topic C: The Dreamweaver CS5 interface

This topic covers the following Adobe ACA exam objectives for Dreamweaver CS5.

#	Objective
3.1a	Identify and label elements of the Dreamweaver interface.
3.1c	Demonstrate knowledge of the Workspace Switcher.
3.2a	Identify types of content that can be created or inserted by using the Insert bar.
3.2b	Demonstrate knowledge of how to change between the categories on the Insert bar.
3.2c	Demonstrate knowledge of how to toggle between "Show as Tabs" and "Show as Menu" on the Insert bar.
3.3a	Demonstrate knowledge of the various functions of the Property inspector.
3.5a	Identify uses of the Files panel.
3.6a	Demonstrate how to open, minimize, collapse, close, resize, dock, and undock panels; how to access preset workspaces; how to change document views; and how to save a custom workspace.
5.3i	Demonstrate knowledge of how to apply emphasis to text by using the Insert menu or the Property inspector.
5.6a	Demonstrate knowledge of HTML tags.

Developing Web sites in Dreamweaver CS5

Explanation

Dreamweaver CS5 makes it easy to design and create Web sites and applications. When you create or change a page in the Dreamweaver workspace, Dreamweaver automatically generates the required XHTML, CSS, or scripting code. You can also write or edit code manually. Before you get started creating Web sites, you should become familiar with the Dreamweaver CS5 interface.

Starting Dreamweaver and opening a file

When you start Dreamweaver, the welcome screen appears, as shown in Exhibit 1-3. Under Create New, you can click any option to open a new blank file of the selected type. For example, click HTML to open a new, blank HTML page. You can start building from this blank page, or you can close it and open an existing file. If you don't want the welcome screen to appear the next time you start Dreamweaver, check "Don't show again" (at the bottom of the screen), and click OK.

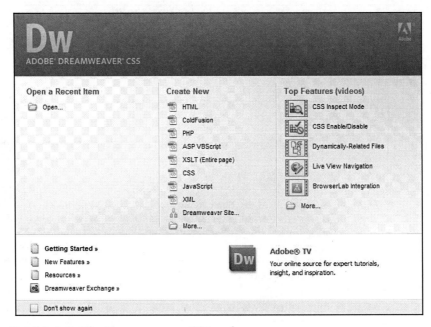

Exhibit 1-3: The Dreamweaver CS5 welcome screen

To open a file, choose File, Open and browse to locate the file you want to open. Select the file and click Open, or double-click the file. To start a new file, choose File, New. The New Document dialog box opens, with the blank HTML page option selected by default. Click Create to start a new HTML page.

Interface components

The default Dreamweaver CS5 interface, shown in Exhibit 1-4, includes the Application bar at the top of the window, the Document toolbar, the Document window (where you perform most of your work), the panel groups (which include the Files panel shown in the bottom-right corner), and the Property inspector (also called the Properties panel).

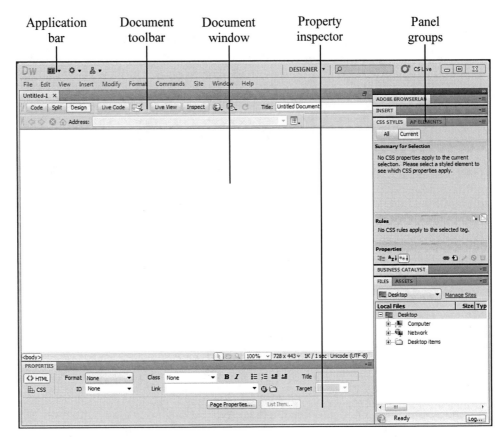

Exhibit 1-4: The Dreamweaver CS5 interface

The following table describes the main components of the Dreamweaver CS5 interface.

Component	Description
ACA objective 3.1a Application bar	Contains application controls, the Workspace Switcher, and menus.
Document toolbar	Provides buttons you can use to perform a variety of common tasks. For example, you can switch between views, check for errors, and enable and disable various visual aids.
Document window	Displays the current page. This is where you'll do most of your work. You can switch among Design, Code, Split, Live, and Live Code views.
Panel groups	Contain a set of panels. Panels contain collections of related options and commands to help you monitor and edit your files. For example, two frequently used panels are the Insert panel and the Files panel.
ACA objective 3.2a Insert panel (or Insert bar)	Provides buttons you can use to quickly insert elements, such as images, links, tables, and Div tags, into a document. You can convert the Insert panel into a horizontal bar for quick access to frequently used elements.
ACA objective 3.5a Files panel	Displays your site folders and files. You can open a file by double-clicking it in the Files panel, or move files by dragging them between folders. You can also drag a file from the Files panel to the Document window to open it, and you can rename, delete, and copy files from within the Files panel.
ACA objective 3.3a Property inspector	(Also called the Properties panel.) Displays the properties of the selected element. The options and commands that appear change based on what's selected in the Document window.

Visual aids

Visual aids are page icons, symbols, or borders that are visible only in Dreamweaver to help you work precisely. You can turn individual visual aids on and off to make it easier to work with your page elements. To set your visual aids, select them from the Visual Aid list on the Document toolbar, as shown in Exhibit 1-5. To toggle all visual aids on or off, press Ctrl+Shift+I.

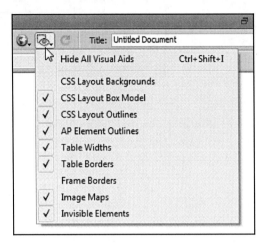

Exhibit 1-5: The Visual Aids list on the Document toolbar

The Zoom tool

The Zoom tool is the magnifying-glass icon at the bottom of the Document window. It allows you to quickly zoom in and out on your pages. Click anywhere on a page to "zoom in," or magnify that area. To zoom out, hold down the Alt key and click the page. You can also drag a marquee around a specific area of a page to zoom in on that area, or you can enter or select a magnification value in the Set magnification box.

Do it!

C-1: Identifying interface components

The files for this activity are in Student Data folder **Unit 1\Topic C**.

If the program shortcut appears in the Start list, tell students to click it to start the program.

Here's how	Here's why
1 Click **Start** and choose **All Programs, Adobe Dreamweaver CS5**	To start Dreamweaver CS5. If the Default Editor dialog box appears, click OK.
2 At the bottom of the welcome screen, check **Don't show again**	To prevent the welcome screen from appearing the next time Dreamweaver CS5 starts. A dialog box appears, indicating that you can enable the welcome screen again later if necessary.
Click **OK**	

TIPS
Students can also press Ctrl+O.

3 Choose **File, Open...**

Browse to the current topic folder	It is in the current unit folder in the Student Data folder.
Open the **Outlander Spices** folder	
Double-click **index.html**	To open the Outlander Spices home page in Split view, the default view in Dreamweaver CS5. You'll switch to Design view for most of this course.

Tell students they will work in Design view for most of this course.

4 On the Document toolbar, click **Design**, as shown

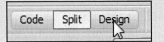

To switch to Design view.

5 On the menu bar, click **File**

To open the File menu. The drop-down menus in the menu bar contain commands for performing a wide variety of tasks.

With the menu open, point to **Edit**

(The next item in the menu bar.) To display the commands in the Edit menu.

Point to **View**

To display the commands in the View menu.

Briefly explore the other menus

ACA objective 3.1a

6 Locate the Address bar

(At the top of the Document window.) As with a browser, the Address bar shows the full path to the open file for reference and verification.

7 At the top of the Panel groups, click **Insert**, as shown

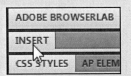

To expand the Insert panel. Using the Insert panel, you can quickly add elements to a page. The buttons in this panel are shortcuts to the commands in the Insert menu.

Double-click **Insert**

To collapse the panel.

8 Locate the Document toolbar

The Document toolbar contains buttons that control the current view of the open Web page. The toolbar also displays the page title and provides buttons and pop-up menus for frequently used commands.

ACA objective 3.3a

9 Locate the Property inspector

The Property inspector displays attributes and options for the selected page element. You can quickly edit properties such as text alignment and font styles.

ACA objective 3.5a

10	Locate the Files panel	The Files panel displays your site folders and files. You can open a file by double-clicking it in the Files panel.
11	On the Document toolbar, click [eye icon]	To display the Visual Aid list.
	From the list, select **Table Borders**	To hide all table borders used in the layout. These are layout guides only; they are not displayed in a browser.
12	Show the table borders again	From the Visual Aid list, select Table Borders.
13	Click [magnifier icon]	The Zoom tool is at the bottom of the Document window.
	Click as shown	

To zoom in on the spice image at the top of the page.

14	Press and hold (ALT)	
	Click the spice image again	To zoom out.
	Release (ALT)	
15	Drag over the green pepper image	To create a marquee
	Release the mouse button	To zoom in on that area of the image.

The values shown here might be different from the values on students' screens.

16	Click as shown	[magnifier] 292% ▾ 785 x 419 ▾ 107K / — Set magnification

(In the lower-right corner of the Document window.) To display the Set magnification list.

Be sure that students return to the default magnification level.

	Select **100%**	To return to the default magnification level.
17	Click [arrow icon]	(At the bottom of the Document window.) The Select tool is the default tool.

Workspace layouts

Explanation

Dreamweaver CS5 provides eight preset workspace layouts designed to suit different types of developers or projects. The layouts are Designer (the default workspace), Designer Compact, App Developer, App Developer Plus, Classic, Coder, Coder Plus, and Dual Screen. Each layout is optimized for its purpose. For example, the Coder workspace is for developers who need to edit code and use code snippets and other assets. You can also create a custom workspace to suit your development preferences.

The Workspace Switcher

ACA objective 3.1c

To switch workspace layouts, click the Workspace Switcher button in the Application bar and choose a layout from the menu, as shown in Exhibit 1-6.

ACA objective 3.6a

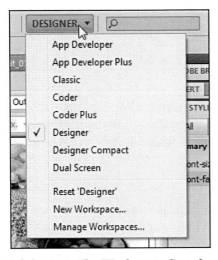

Exhibit 1-6: The Workspace Switcher

Custom workspaces

ACA objective 3.6a

In addition to using the default workspace layouts, you can arrange any workspace layout to suit your specific needs and save that layout for repeated use. To create a custom workspace layout:

1　Arrange the panels and toolbars in the workspace as desired.
2　From the Workspace Switcher menu, choose New Workspace to open the New Workspace dialog box.
3　Enter a descriptive name for the workspace and click OK. The new workspace name appears at the top of the Application bar.

You can rename or delete custom workspaces by choosing Manage Workspaces from the Workspace Switcher menu. This opens the Manage Workspaces dialog box, which contains a list of custom workspaces (if any).

Panel groups in the Designer workspace layout

Each workspace layout has its own set and arrangement of panels. The Designer workspace layout displays two panel groups by default: Files and CSS Styles. You can open additional panels in any workspace layout.

The Files panel group

ACA objective 3.5a

The Files panel group, shown in Exhibit 1-7, contains the Files panel and the Assets panel. The Files panel allows you to quickly open and manage site files and folders. The Assets panel provides easy access to your site assets, such as images, templates, PDFs, and media files. To use the Assets panel, you must first define a local site.

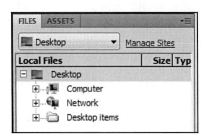

Exhibit 1-7: The Files panel group, with the Files panel active

The CSS Styles panel group

The CSS Styles panel group contains the CSS Styles panel and the AP Elements panel. The CSS Styles panel is context-sensitive, allowing you to manage the CSS (Cascading Style Sheet) styles of the selected element. With the AP Elements panel, you can manage properties of absolutely positioned elements (most commonly, `<div>` tags).

Rearranging panels

You can show, hide, and rearrange panels to customize your workspace. To hide or display a panel group, choose Window and then choose a panel group. To expand or collapse a panel group, double-click its title bar. To undock, or "float," a panel group, drag it by its title bar to a desired location. To resize a floating panel, point to one of its edges so that the pointer changes to a double-sided arrow; then drag to resize the panel.

To dock a floating panel, drag it above or below an existing panel. A blue line will appear, indicating where the panel will be docked when you release the mouse button.

You can reset a modified workspace to its original layout by choosing Reset *'Workspace Name'* (for instance, Reset 'Coder') from the Workspace Switcher menu.

Converting the Insert panel to a horizontal Insert bar

ACA objectives 3.2a, 3.2b, 3.2c

You can convert the Insert panel to a horizontal bar for quick access to frequently used elements and commands. To do so, drag the Insert panel tab above the Document window. A blue line appears, indicating where the Insert bar will be placed. Release the mouse button to place the Insert bar.

By default, the Insert bar appears as a row of tabs that provide access to related commands. To switch the Insert bar from a tab-based layout to a single bar with a menu for switching categories, right-click the Insert bar and choose Show as Menu. The default category is Common; it includes frequently used elements such as links, tables, and images. To switch back to a tabbed layout, click Common (or the currently selected category) and choose Show as Tabs.

To convert the Insert bar back to a panel, drag from its gripper (the row of small dots) and drop it where your panels are docked.

C-2:   **Customizing your workspace**

Here's how	Here's why

1 Double-click where shown

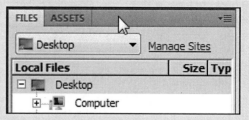

(Be sure to click the blank area and not the Assets tab.) To collapse the panel. Collapsing this panel shows more of CSS Styles panel.

Click the **Files** tab

To expand the Files panel. (You can also double-click the blank area at the top of the Files panel again.)

2 Right-click **Business Catalyst**

(In the Panel groups.) To display a shortcut menu.

Choose **Close**

To close the panel.

3 To the right of Adobe Browserlab, click as shown

To display a menu.

Choose **Close**

4 Point to the right edge of the Document window, as shown

The pointer changes to a double-sided arrow, indicating that you can resize the window.

Drag to the right

To enlarge the Document window and narrow the panels slightly.

5 Expand the Insert panel

6 Drag the CSS Styles panel to the Document window

To make it a floating panel.

Collapse the CSS Styles panel

Double-click the blank area to the right of the AP Elements tab.

7 Drag the collapsed CSS Styles panel above the Files panel

(And below the Insert panel.) A blue line shows precisely where the panel group will be placed.

8 From the Workspace Switcher menu, choose
New Workspace...

To open the New Workspace dialog box.

Type **My workspace**

Click **OK**

The workspace name appears as the active workspace on the Application bar.

9 From the Workspace Switcher menu, choose **Designer Compact**

In this workspace layout, the panels are reduced to buttons on the right side of the window.

10 Click as shown

To display the Insert panel as a flyout panel.

Click the **Files** button

To display the Files panel.

Click the **Files** button again

To close it.

11 Point as shown

These dotted lines are called the "gripper." You can drag from the gripper to move items in the workspace.

Drag the Insert button above the Document window

To place the Insert bar.

12 Right-click the **Common** tab

Choose **Show as Menu**

To streamline the Insert bar. The Common category is displayed by default.

Click **Common**

To open the menu of categories.

Choose **Text**

To view the elements in the Text category. From here, you can quickly insert HTML tags that apply to text.

Tell students they will develop their own workspace preferences as they become more familiar with using the program.

13	Click **Text**	To open the menu.
	Choose **Show as Tabs**	To switch back to a tabbed Insert bar.
14	From the Workspace Switcher menu, choose **Reset 'Designer Compact'**	The Insert commands switch back to the flyout panel on the right side.
15	From the Workspace Switcher menu, choose **My workspace**	To switch back to your custom workspace.

The Property inspector

Explanation

The Property inspector (also called the Properties panel) displays the options and properties of the element that's selected in the Document window. For example, if you select an image on the page, the Property inspector displays the image's properties, such as its height and width, as shown in Exhibit 1-8. You can use the Property inspector to observe properties and to set or modify properties.

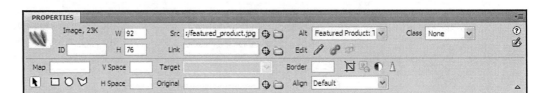

Exhibit 1-8: The Property inspector, with an image selected

ACA objectives 3.3a, 5.3i

For example, you can select a paragraph of text and use the Property inspector to apply basic formatting such as emphasis (boldface or italics), or to assign a class or ID. You can also use the Property inspector to create links and modify tables and image maps.

When you select page elements (other than embedded objects like images and videos), the Property inspector displays two buttons on the left side: HTML and CSS. By default, HTML options are displayed. Click CSS to display the CSS-related options for a selected element.

Do it!

C-3: Working with the Property inspector

Here's how	Here's why
1 On the page, click **In the News**	You'll use the Property inspector to view the attributes for this text.
ACA objective 3.3a Observe the Property inspector	It shows that this text is defined as a heading and does not have an assigned class or ID.
2 On the left side of the Property inspector, click **CSS**	To display the CSS (Cascading Style Sheet) properties assigned to this text. The font, font size, and text color are displayed.
Click **HTML**	(On the left side of the Property inspector.) To display the HTML-related properties for the selected element. You could make the text a link and apply other basic HTML attributes.
3 Click the image shown	To select it.
Observe the Property inspector	It displays the attributes and options for the selected image.
Point out that this is just to show how students can easily customize their environment as they work. 4 Double-click to the right of the Properties tab, as shown	To hide the Property inspector and display more of the Document window.
Show the Property inspector again	Double-click the area to the right of the Properties tab.
5 Scroll down the page	In the Document window.
Under Awards, drag to select **highest quality**, as shown	
ACA objectives 5.3i, 5.6a In the Property inspector, click as shown	To apply emphasis (italics) to the selection. Dreamweaver uses the `<em>` tag to create the emphasis.

6 Click **Awards**

To place the insertion point.

Click **CSS**

(In the Property inspector.) To display the style properties of the selected element. With this option selected, styles that you apply will be created in the style sheet rather than using HTML tags.

7 Click the Color box, as shown

To open a color palette. The pointer changes to an eyedropper, which you can use to select a color.

Applying color is covered elsewhere in the course.

Click the dark green color shown

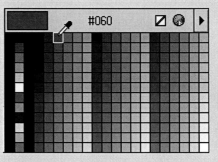

To match the color of the other headings on the page. The text color is now dark green.

TIPS *Students can also press Ctrl+S or choose File, Save to save the document.*

8 Choose **File**, **Close**

Click **Yes**

To save your changes in index.html

Click **Yes**

To save your changes in the style sheet.

Topic D: Basic editing

This topic covers the following Adobe ACA exam objectives for Dreamweaver CS5.

#	Objective
1.4a	Define website accessibility.
1.4c	Explain why including accessibility in website design matters to clients and the target audience.
1.4d	Identify elements of an HTML page that can be read by screen readers.
2.4c	Identify specific techniques used to make a website accessible to viewers with visual and motor impairments.
2.4d	Identify elements of a website that by default are not read by screen readers.
4.3a	Demonstrate knowledge of how to add text to an HTML page.
4.4a	Demonstrate knowledge of the steps for inserting images.
4.4b	Demonstrate knowledge of how to add alternative text to images, using the Image Tag Accessibility Attributes dialog box or the Property inspector.
6.1c	Demonstrate knowledge of how to preview a Web page in a browser.

Editing content

Explanation

Adding and editing content in Design view is similar to using a word processor. You can click on the page to place the insertion point, and type to insert text. You can also edit, delete, and rearrange text, and insert images and media files.

Typical page elements

Web pages can include many types of content, including text, tables, images, and links, as shown in Exhibit 1-9.

Links —

Image —

Text —

Exhibit 1-9: A sample Web page

The following table describes some typical Web page elements.

Element	Description
Text	Words, phrases, sentences, headings, and paragraphs.
Table	A grid structure consisting of rows and columns, meant primarily to contain tabular data, such as a product list with corresponding prices. Tables can also help you control the layout and spacing of elements on a page, although CSS is generally regarded as the superior method for controlling layout.
Image	A graphic file, typically in .gif, .jpg, or .png format. Images can also be used as links.
Link	Text or an image that directs the browser to another location or resource when clicked. The destination might be another Web page, another area of the current page, or a file such as a PDF or Excel document.
Image map	A single graphic that can include multiple links.
Forms	Interactive pages consisting of text input fields, check boxes, and buttons that allow users to submit data to a server for processing and data storage.

Do it!

D-1: Discussing Web page elements

Questions and answers
Facilitate a brief discussion for each item.

1 What are links?

   A link can be text or an image that takes users to another location or resource when clicked.

2 What's the difference between an image and an image map?

   An image is a graphic on a Web page. An image can act as a link, or it can be a static visual element with no functionality. An image map is an image that contains multiple links to various locations.

> 3 What's a table used for?
>
>   *Answers may vary. Tables are primarily meant to contain tabular data, but they can also be used to control the layout and spacing of elements on a page.*
>
> 4 Have you ever used a form on the Internet? If so, for what purpose?
>
>   *Answers will vary. If you have ever become a member of an online organization, bank, or store, you have used a form to enter your personal information.*

Text basics

Explanation

To add text to a page, you can simply type at the insertion point, or you can copy and paste text from another source. Inserting and editing text can sometimes cause other elements on the page to move. For example, an image below a paragraph will move down as you add more text to the paragraph.

Do it!

D-2: Inserting and editing text

The files for this activity are in Student Data folder **Unit 1\Topic D**.

Here's how	Here's why
1 Press CTRL + O	The Open dialog box is displayed.
Browse to the current topic folder	
In the Outlander Spices folder, open index.html	
2 In the top paragraph, click to the left of **spices**, as shown	heritage of |spices from all id specialty stores all over To place the insertion point at this location.
3 Type **the finest**	To add text to the paragraph.
Press SPACEBAR	To add a space. This type of text editing is similar to working in a word processor.
4 Place the insertion point as shown	**Featured Products|** Only one product is currently featured, so you'll delete the "s" in "Products."
Press ← BACKSPACE	To delete the letter "s."
5 Press CTRL + S	To update the document.

Tell students to ignore the Code Navigator icon that appears near the insertion point.

ACA objective 4.3a

Point out that when you add text to a text block that has styles already applied, as it does here, the new text uses the same styles.

TIPS ✓ *Students can also choose File, Save.*

Adding images

Explanation

You can use images to convey or reinforce ideas in ways that text alone cannot. A Web page that includes images is often more visually appealing and inviting to the user than is a page with just text.

ACA objective 4.4a

To insert an image in a Web page:

1 If necessary, create a subfolder in the site folder and place all the image files in it. Give the folder a logical name, such as "images."

2 In the Files panel, navigate to the folder containing the images for the current site.

ACA objective 4.4b

3 Drag an image file to the Document window.

4 In the Image Tag Accessibility Attributes dialog box, type a meaningful text alternative and click OK.

You can then adjust the size and position of an image by using the options in the Property inspector. In the Property inspector, you can also add or modify alternate text by using the Alt box.

Accessibility and alternate text

ACA objectives 1.4a, 1.4c

When you add an image, Dreamweaver prompts you to provide alternate text for it. Doing this is important for ensuring accessibility. Accessible Web design entails using simple methods that help make your content operable on a variety of devices, beyond the standard visual browsers like Internet Explorer, Safari, Firefox, and Chrome.

ACA objectives 1.4d, 2.4c, 2.4d

For example, users with visual impairments are likely to use alternative browsing devices such as screen readers and Braille printers. These devices can access any text content, but they can't read or describe an image, so they rely on the text alternative that you specify. Alternate text should describe either the content or the purpose of the image, whichever is most appropriate.

It's important to make an effort to ensure that your site content is accessible to these devices. Doing so can also help to establish a loyal user base.

D-3: Adding an image

The files for this activity are in Student Data folder **Unit 1\Topic D**.

Here's how	Here's why
1 Scroll to the bottom of the page	You'll insert an image to the left of the Awards heading.
2 In the Files panel, expand Desktop items	Click the plus sign next to it.
3 Open the Student Data folder	Double-click it.
Open the current unit folder	
Open the current topic folder	
4 In the Outlander Spices folder, open the images folder	
Scroll down in the list of images to find iso.gif	

Here's how	Here's why
5 Drag **iso.gif** to the left of the Awards heading, as shown	
	To insert the image on the page. The Image Tag Accessibility Attributes dialog box opens.
In the Alternate text box, type **ISO 9000 Award**	Providing a text alternative ensures that users with non-visual browsers can access the content.
Click **OK**	To close the Image Tag Accessibility Attributes dialog box.
6 Save the page	Press Ctrl+S.

Previewing a Web page

Explanation

As you work on a page, you'll probably want to periodically see it as it will appear in a browser. To preview a Web page in a browser:

ACA objective 6.1c

1 On the Document toolbar, click the "Preview/Debug in browser" button.
2 From the drop-down list, select a browser.
3 If you have not yet saved your changes, a dialog box opens, prompting you to save your changes. Click Yes to save your changes and preview the page in the selected browser.

Adding browsers to the Preview list

Not all browsers display a Web page the same way—there are often minor differences in how each browser interprets HTML and CSS code, and these differences can affect the way a page looks and functions. For this reason, it's a good idea to preview your Web pages in several popular browsers. When you first install Dreamweaver, it detects the browsers installed on your computer. It uses your default browser as the primary browser for previewing pages. You can add other browsers as needed.

To add other browsers to the Preview list:

1 On the Document toolbar, click the "Preview/Debug in browser" button and choose Edit Browser List to open the Preferences dialog box. (You can also choose Edit, Preferences or press Ctrl+U to open the Preferences dialog box.)
2 In the Category list, select Preview in Browser.
3 Click the plus sign next to Browsers to open the Add Browser dialog box.
4 In the Name box, type a name for the browser.
5 Click the Browse button, and navigate to the .exe file for the desired browser (typically located in a folder in the C:\Program Files folder).
6 Check Secondary browser.
7 Click OK to close the Add Browser dialog box.
8 Repeat steps 3–7 for each browser you want to add to the Preview list.
9 Click OK to close the Preferences dialog box.

Do it!

D-4: Previewing a page in a browser

ACA objective 6.1c

Tell students that another browser might be listed first if Internet Explorer isn't the default browser on their PCs or if another browser has been defined as the Primary browser in Preferences. The browser might be listed as iexplore or IEXPLORE.EXE, depending on how the PC was configured.

Here's how	Here's why
1 On the Document toolbar, click [icon]	(The "Preview/Debug in browser" button.) To display a list of options.
Select **Preview in IExplore**	To view the page in Internet Explorer. A dialog box might open, prompting you to save your changes in the style sheet.
Click **Yes**	(If necessary.) To update the style sheet.
2 Verify your changes and close the browser	
3 In Dreamweaver, close index.html	

Unit summary: Getting started

Topic A   In this topic, you learned about the Internet, the Web, and HTML. You learned that HTML and XHTML are standard **markup languages** used to build Web pages, and that Dreamweaver uses XHTML code by default.

Topic B   In this topic, you learned about basic **project management** concepts. You learned about the phases of a project lifecycle and the typical problems that can threaten the success of a project. You also learned about the important role that effective **communication** and **planning** have in making any Web development project a success.

Topic C   In this topic, you identified the main components of the **Dreamweaver CS5 workspace**, including the Document window, Property inspector, and panel groups. You learned how to switch between **workspace layouts** and create a custom workspace.

Topic D   In this topic, you learned how to perform basic **text editing**, and you learned how to insert an **image** and provide a text alternative. You learned that providing alternate text is an important component of accessible design. You also learned how to **preview** a page in a browser.

Independent practice activity

In this activity, you'll insert an image, specify alternate text, apply basic text formatting, and preview the page in Internet Explorer.

The files for this activity are in Student Data folder **Unit 1\Unit summary**.

1 Open index.html.

2 In the empty area to the left of the first paragraph, insert the peppers.jpg image. (It's in the images folder.)

3 Provide the text alternative **Chili peppers**.

4 Drag to select the text "Discover a whole new world of flavor:"

5 Using the Property inspector, make the text bold. (*Hint:* Select HTML and click the B button.)

6 Save the page and preview it in Internet Explorer.

7 Close the browser to return to Dreamweaver.

8 Close all open files.

Review questions

1 How can you hide table borders?

   A Right-click inside the table and choose Table, Hide Table Borders.

   B Double-click the table border.

   C Select the table and choose View, Hide Table Borders.

   D Deselect the Table Borders option in the Visual Aids list on the Document toolbar.

2 Name some design factors that are important to analyze and plan before you get started on a Web development project.

   Answers may vary. All design and development factors should be a part of the planning phase of a Web development project. This includes establishing the navigational structure, the color and font scheme, the amount of content per page, the intended audience, and so on.

3 True or false? The properties and options that are displayed in the Property inspector changed based on what is selected in the Document window.

   True.

4 How can you add an image to a page?

   A Drag the image file from the Files panel to the Document window.

   B In the Files panel, right-click the image and choose Insert.

   C Choose File, Import; navigate to the location of the image file; and click OK.

   D In the Files panel, double-click the image file.

5 Why is it important to always specify a text alternative when you insert an image?

   Alternative browsing devices such as screen readers and Braille printers can't read or describe an image, so they rely on the text alternative you specify.

Unit 2

Web sites and pages

Unit time: 75 minutes

Complete this unit, and you'll know how to:

A Use planning tools such as flowcharts, storyboards, and wireframes, and identify and apply basic principles of design.

B Define a local site, work with the Files panel and the Assets panel, create pages, import text from external files, and set page properties.

C Identify basic HTML tags, switch between document views, work with code and the code tools, insert special characters, and use the Find and Replace dialog box to update content and code.

Topic A: Planning tools and design principles

This topic covers the following Adobe ACA exam objectives for Dreamweaver CS5.

#	Objective
2.1a	Identify attributes of a website that demonstrate consistency.
2.1c	Identify the benefits of consistency.
2.3a	Demonstrate knowledge of graphic design elements and principles.
2.3b	Identify examples of horizontal symmetry, vertical symmetry, diagonal symmetry, radial symmetry, and asymmetric layouts.
2.3c	Recognize examples of page designs that violate design principles or best practices.
2.4a	List elements used to improve website usability.
2.4b	Demonstrate knowledge of text formatting guidelines that improve readability.
2.5a	Demonstrate knowledge of flowcharts.
2.5b	Demonstrate knowledge of storyboards.
2.5c	List items that appear on a website design storyboard.
2.5d	Demonstrate knowledge of wireframes.
2.5e	Recognize a website that follows a planned website hierarchy.

Planning the site structure and design

Explanation

You've already explored basic site planning concepts. Next you'll learn about some common planning and organizational tools and methods you can apply to plan your site before you start building it. Organizing site files in a logical structure is a critical part of this process. A good site structure makes it easier to maintain the site efficiently over time.

Think about how best to structure your pages and content, how you want to present information, and how you want the site to look (color schemes, fonts, and so on) before you begin the actual work. Because content requirements, design changes, and job assignments typically change over time, you should plan and design a site that is easy to maintain and easy to transfer to another developer or team of developers.

Planning tools

Flowcharts, storyboards, and wireframes are effective planning tools that you can use individually or with a group to help map out and visualize your site plan.

Flowcharts

ACA objective 2.5a

A well-designed site must have an effective navigation scheme. You need to plan the link relationships between the pages in your site. Sometimes you can prevent problems by drafting a site flowchart, similar to the simple example shown in Exhibit 2-1.

ACA objective 2.4a

Keeping a flowchart up-to-date as you build your site can also help you create a site map when you're ready to publish the site. A *site map* is like a table of contents for a site. It should provide the visitor with links to the main topics or sections in the site and reveal the site's content hierarchy. In this way, site maps enhance the usability of a site, especially if the site is complex or contains a lot of information.

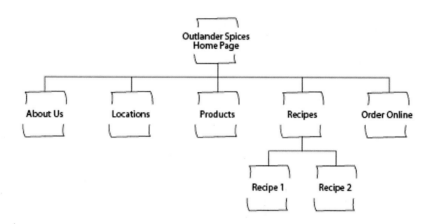

Exhibit 2-1: A simple flowchart for the Outlander Spices site

Storyboards

ACA objective 2.5b

Storyboards were used by early creators of animated movies to plan and visualize a story before beginning the actual drawing for the film. Storyboards were, in effect, still drawings that made up a summary or outline of the film. For Web development projects, using a storyboard can help you generate and organize ideas for your site. Storyboards can be as simple as sketches on index cards or a white board, or as detailed as colored illustrations and computer graphics.

ACA objective 2.5c

Just as storyboards lay the foundation for an animation, you can use them to brainstorm ideas for how users will interact with your site. For example, you can design the steps users will take to access certain information or proceed through a series of interactive forms. Storyboards typically include arrows indicating the intended flow of activity, the branching of screens that result in each possible step, notes to describe the designed action, and lists of support files, such as graphics file names, content sources, or the names of people or departments responsible for creating certain components.

During development, checking your work against an approved storyboard can help keep you on track, and it can help keep a team's efforts focused and well coordinated.

Wireframes

ACA objective 2.5d

A wireframe is similar to a flowchart in that it provides a visual guide for the creation of a Web site, showing link relationships between pages and the general hierarchy of information. However, a wireframe is more of a design mockup—a template that shows the placement of page elements like logos, navigation bars, major content sections, and so on. Wireframes act as a sort of skeleton for a site and help you maintain design consistency across all site pages.

You can create multiple wireframes depicting layout and design variations, enabling participants to brainstorm ideas and offer suggestions. Wireframes help you visualize what the finished product will look like so that you and/or the project team can review and critique it before the bulk of the work is done. Adobe Fireworks is a popular software tool for creating wireframes, as well as site graphics and actual pages.

Do it!

A-1: Discussing planning tools

Here's how	**Here's why**

Facilitate a brief discussion for each item.

ACA objective 2.5a

1 How can creating a flowchart help you build a site?

A flowchart can help you visualize your site's navigation scheme and the link relationships between pages. Keeping a flowchart up-to-date as you build your site can also help you create a site map when you're ready to publish the site.

ACA objective 2.5b

2 How might a storyboard help you plan a site or an application within a site?

Answers may vary. A storyboard can help you design the steps users will take to access certain information or proceed through a series of interactive forms.

ACA objective 2.5c

3 What sorts of elements might appear on a storyboard?

Answers may vary but could include arrows indicating the intended flow of activity, the branching of screens that result in each possible step, notes to describe the designed action, and lists of support files, such as graphics file names, content sources, or the names of people or departments responsible for creating certain components.

ACA objective 2.5d

4 How might using wireframes help you build and optimize a site layout?

Answers may vary. By using wireframes, you can create design mockups that show the placement of key page elements, like logos, navigation bars, and content sections. Wireframes can help you visualize how the finished product might look and gather feedback and ideas before the bulk of the work is done.

5 Open Internet Explorer

ACA objective 2.5e

You can also have students go to another site of your choice to observe and discuss matters of structure, organization, and consistency.

6 In the Address bar, type
http://www.wikipedia.org

Press (↵ ENTER)   To go to the Wikipedia site.

7 Click **English**

Click **All portals**

Click an item of interest

Observe how the information is structured

8 Do you think the site structures information in a logical and effective hierarchy? Why or why not?

Answers may vary.

9 Close Internet Explorer

Basic design principles

Explanation

Even before it was possible to use rich media on the Web, developers too often went overboard with design elements, combining too many fonts and colors and using unnecessary animations, in an attempt to make things interesting. But too much styling, especially styling without any real purpose, can make a site confusing, garish, and difficult to read. A well-designed, professional-looking site should not annoy its users. Even without professional graphic design training, you can make your pages effective by employing clean, simple styles.

ACA objective 2.3a

An in-depth discussion of graphic design is beyond the scope of this course, but you should be familiar with the following basic principles of design and composition.

- **Emphasis** — Which page elements draw your eye the most or attract attention? You might find, after you've worked on a page, that the answers to these questions aren't what you had planned.

ACA objective 2.3b

- **Symmetry** — People tend to notice symmetry and it can be subconsciously pleasing. Consider using symmetry (horizontal, vertical, diagonal, or radial) in your layout, color choices, or graphic elements.

- **White space** — White space (meaning empty space, not necessarily white) between text and images can be an important part of a layout. White space contributes significantly to design appeal and the readability of text.

- **Color and contrast** — It's critical that you choose color combinations that are easy on the eyes and easy to read. Contrast is a critical component of text readability. If there is insufficient contrast between the text color and its background color, it can strain the eyes.

Consistency

ACA objectives 2.1a, 2.1c, 2.4a

It's also critical to maintain a consistent look and feel across an entire site. Users should have no doubt that they are still on your site when they click a link to a different page. Use consistent navigation and layouts throughout the site to prevent confusion. Persistent links should be in the same place on all pages to make it easy to navigate.

Also, the color scheme should be consistent across the site. This enhances brand identity as well as site identity. Choose colors that are easy on the eyes. If you want to use different colors to distinguish various sections of the site, it's even more important to keep other layout elements consistent. Clarity and consistency make a site more readable and usable, and can make life easier for the developer and administrator, allowing for faster development and easier maintenance.

Readability

ACA objectives 2.4a, 2.4b

Great content is wasted if users can't easily read it. The following general guidelines can help you ensure that your text and graphics are readable.

- Use only a few fonts on the site. Choose fonts that are easily readable and are appropriate for the content (e.g., don't use Comic Sans if you want to be taken seriously).

- Don't make your text too small. Remember that everything will look smaller on a screen set to a higher resolution.

- Use white space to help make text clear and readable. Don't crowd elements together or try to fit too much into a page or section.

- Be sure there is sufficient contrast between the text and background colors.

- Ask volunteers to help you test the readability of your text.

Do it! **A-2: Discussing design factors and principles**

Questions and answers

ACA objective 2.3a

1 Name a few important aspects of effective site design.

Answers may vary, but could include:

- **Effective use of color and contrast**
- **Effective use of white space**
- **Consistency of layout**

ACA objective 2.4b

2 Name a few things you can do to help ensure that your content is readable.

Answers may vary, but could include:

- **Don't use too many different fonts.**
- **Use easily readable fonts that are large enough even for high-resolution screens.**
- **Use white space to make pages clear and readable. Don't crowd elements.**
- **Be sure there is sufficient contrast between the text color and the background color.**
- **Ask volunteers to help you test the readability of your text.**

ACA objective 2.1c

3 List some benefits of a consistent look and feel across a site.

Answers may vary, but could include:

- **It enhances brand identity and site identity.**
- **It prevents confusion and potential navigation problems.**
- **Sites that are consistently designed are easier to update and maintain.**

ACA objective 2.3b

Ask for student volunteers and briefly visit each site and point out the use of each type of symmetry.

ACA objective 2.3c

Ask for a student volunteer and have him or her visit the site and briefly discuss its design limitations.

4 Follow your instructor's lead to view and discuss examples of site designs that make use of horizontal symmetry, vertical symmetry, diagonal symmetry, radial symmetry, and asymmetric layouts.

5 Name an example of a site design that violates key design principles, and point out its limitations.

Examples will vary. Make note of known Web sites or good examples offered by students.

Topic B: Defining and building a site

This topic covers the following Adobe ACA exam objectives for Dreamweaver CS5.

#	Objective
3.4a	Demonstrate knowledge of the Site and Favorites lists on the Assets panel.
3.4b	Identify types of content that can be accessed by using the Assets panel.
3.4c	Demonstrate knowledge of how to apply assets from the Assets panel to a Web page.
3.5a	Identify uses of the Files panel.
4.1a	Demonstrate knowledge of the terms "local site," "remote site/folder," "Web server," and "root folder."
4.1b	Demonstrate knowledge of the steps for defining a new Dreamweaver site.
4.2a	Demonstrate knowledge of the steps used to create, save, and name a new HTML page.
4.2b	Demonstrate knowledge of rules for naming HTML files.
4.2c	Demonstrate knowledge of best practices for naming HTML files.
4.2d	Identify the result of naming an HTML file "index.htm(l)" or "default.htm(l)".
4.2e	Differentiate between document filenames and document or page titles.
4.2f	Demonstrate knowledge of how to assign a document or page title.
4.3a	Demonstrate knowledge of how to add text to an HTML page.
4.10a	Demonstrate knowledge of how to add Word or Excel content to a Web page.
4.10b	Demonstrate knowledge of the correct settings to use when importing a Word document, based on the content in the document.
5.1a	Identify document properties that can be set or edited globally by using the Page Properties dialog box.
6.5a	Demonstrate knowledge of how to delete files by using the Files panel.
6.5b	Demonstrate knowledge of how to rename files and update links by using the Files panel.

Local, remote, and testing sites

Explanation

When you get started on a site, you'll set up a local site folder in which to build your site files. You might also need to establish a testing folder on a Web server if your site includes applications that interact with data. When you're ready to publish your site, you'll upload it to a remote server.

The following table describes local, remote, and testing sites.

Folder	Location	Purpose
ACA objective 4.1a Local	Your local hard disk	To store work in progress. You can transfer files from the local site to the other sites when they're complete.
Remote	The Web server where your site is published	To make your site available to your intended audience.
Testing	Any computer running the server and application software you need	To test your connection to databases and dynamic pages (pages that change according to information received from databases or page variables).

Defining a local site

The local folder on your computer is where you work on the site before publishing it on the Internet. After you verify that it looks and functions as you intend, you can publish it to a remote folder on the Web server that hosts your site.

ACA objective 4.1a

A local site serves as the root folder for your Web site. (The *root folder* is at the top of the site hierarchy; it contains all other site folders and files.) Any folder on your computer—except your hard drive root directory (C:\) or the Dreamweaver application folder—can serve as the local site folder.

To define a local site:

ACA objective 4.1b

1 Choose Site, New Site to open the Site Setup dialog box, shown in Exhibit 2-2.
2 In the Site name box, enter a name for the site.
3 In the Local Site Folder box, enter the path to the folder or click the folder icon to browse to and select the folder.
4 Click Save. The site files and folders are displayed in the Files panel.

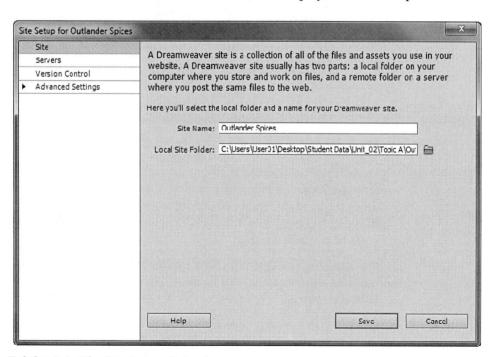

Exhibit 2-2: The Site Setup dialog box

The Files panel

ACA objectives 6.5a, 6.5b

After you define a site, the site files are displayed in the Files panel, along with any subfolders that exist in your root site folder. To open a file from the Files panel, double-click the file. To delete a file from the Files panel (and therefore from the site), select the file, press Delete, and then click Yes to confirm the deletion. To rename a file, click it twice slowly to select the file name; then type the new file name and press Enter.

Organizing site files

You should keep all the files you plan to use in the site in a logical, organized folder structure. For example, Exhibit 2-3 shows a typical folder structure for a simple Web site. All images are stored in their own folder, as are style sheets. You might also have separate folders to store resources such as PDF files, videos, and scripts.

ACA objective 3.5a

Dreamweaver does not create this structure for you when you define a site—you need to organize your files and folders inside your site's root folder before you define the site. You can also create new folders and HTML files directly within the Files panel and then move them as needed, but it's usually best to establish the folder structure in advance. In addition to creating new files and folders, you can also open files, rename files and folders, and delete files and folders.

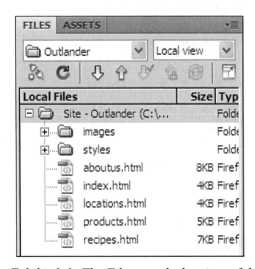

Exhibit 2-3: The Files panel, showing a folder structure for a simple site

The Assets panel

ACA objective 3.4b

You can use the Assets panel to keep track of your site's assets, such as images, colors, scripts, URLs, and videos. By default, the Assets panel, shown in Exhibit 2-4, displays a list of the images in your site and information about each file—its dimensions, file size, file type, and path. You can click the icons on the left side of the panel to view other types of assets in the site.

ACA objective 3.4c

You can drag and drop files from the Assets panel to insert them in a page. This provides an alternate way of locating, organizing, and working with your site files. However, you cannot delete files from within the Assets panel.

By default, assets are listed alphabetically. You can also sort them by size, file type, or other categories by clicking a category's column heading.

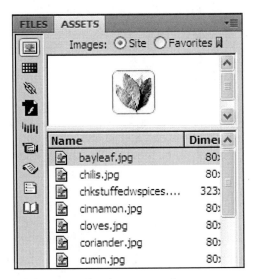

Exhibit 2-4: The Assets panel

Favorite assets

When you're working with a large site with many assets, the list of files can become cumbersome to sort through. By tagging certain assets as favorites, you can view your assets in a shortened list of only important or relevant files, thus making it easier to manage your site resources.

ACA objective 3.4c

To create a list of favorite assets, select one or more assets in the Site list in the Assets panel, and then click the Add To Favorites button at the bottom of the panel. You can also right-click an asset or multiple selected assets, and choose Add To Favorites.

After you add assets to the Favorites list, you can select Favorites to display only those assets. You can also group related assets into folders, or assign nicknames to help you recall the assets' intended use. For example, you can give color assets names that indicate how or where they are used in the site.

Do it!

B-1: Defining a local site and exploring assets

The files for this activity are in Student Data folder **Unit 2\Topic B**.

Here's how	Here's why
ACA objective 4.1b 1 Choose **Site, New Site...**	To open the Site Setup dialog box.
2 In the Site Name box, type **Outlander Spices**	To name the site.
Click as shown	Browse for folder
	To open the Choose Root Folder dialog box.

3	Click **Desktop**	On the left side of the dialog box.
	Open the Student Data folder	
	Open the current unit folder	
4	In the current topic folder, open the Outlander Spices folder	
	Click **Select**	To set the root folder for this site, where the files for the site will be stored.
5	Click **Save**	To define the root site folder.
6	Observe the Files panel	Outlander Spices is the site name.

The size of students' Files panel might be different depending on the size of their screens and any adjustments they have made.

Point out that the images and styles folders were already in the Outlander Spices folder. Dreamweaver does not create site subfolders.

Observe the contents of the Site folder

The Site folder contains several files, as well as an images folder, for storing the site's image files, and a styles folder, for storing style sheets.

7	Click **videoinfo.doc**	(Scroll down in the Files panel, if necessary.) To select it.
	Click it again	(Or press F2.) So that you can rename the file.

Point out that Dreamweaver does not select the file extension by default, so you need only type the file name.

	Type **videos**	To rename the file.
8	At the top of the Files panel group, click **Assets**	To display the Assets panel. By default, it displays the site's images.

ACA objective 6.5b

ACA objective 3.4b

	Click ▦	To display the colors used in the site.
	Click ▨	To display the site's image assets again.

Tell students to scroll to the right, if necessary.

9	Use the horizontal scrollbar to view the image details	(At the bottom of the Assets panel.) You can also detach the panel and enlarge it to see more of the information provided in the Assets panel.

	10 Click any image in the Assets panel	To select it. A preview of the image appears at the top of the panel.
	Select another image	To preview it. The Assets panel provides an alternative to the Files panel for finding specific resources and getting information about them.
Help students find the Name column heading. They might have to scroll back to the left.	11 Click **Name**	(The column heading just above the first image in the list.) To sort the images in reverse alphabetical order.
	Click **Name** again	To sort the images in alphabetical order again.
	12 Select **bayleaf.jpg**	If necessary.
	Press (DELETE)	Nothing happens because you can't delete files from within the Assets panel. To delete or move files, you need to use the Files panel.
ACA objective 3.4c	13 Right-click **bayleaf.jpg** and choose **Locate in Site**	To find this asset in the site. The Files panel is activated, and bayleaf.jpg is selected in the images folder. In larger sites with a lot of assets, this command can help you find files quickly.
	14 Switch to the Assets panel	
	Select **logo.gif**	Scroll down, if necessary.
ACA objective 3.4a	Click as shown	
		(The Add To Favorites button is at the bottom of the Assets panel.) To add the image to the Favorites list.
	Click **OK**	
	15 Display the color assets	
Color codes are covered elsewhere in the course.	16 Select **#99cc33**	The light green color. (This is a hexadecimal value for this color.)
	Add this color to the Favorites list	
	17 Click a color and then hold down the (CTRL) key	
	Click another color	To select two colors. You'll add these colors to the Favorites list.
	Release the (CTRL) key	

18 Right-click the selection and choose **Add to Favorites**	You could also click the Add To Favorites button at the bottom of the Assets panel.
Click **OK**	
19 In the Assets panel, select **Favorites**	To display the favorite assets. Only site resources that you tag as favorites are displayed here. The colors you selected are displayed, but not the image—favorite assets are displayed separately by type.
Click **#99cc33**	You'll assign a nickname to this color.
Type **Navigation bar green**	Nicknames can remind you how various colors are used in the site.
20 Display the favorite images	Logo.gif is selected by default.
Observe the Add To Favorites button	When you're viewing a list of favorites, the button changes to Remove From Favorites, indicated by the minus sign.
Remove logo.gif from the Favorites list	(Click the Remove From Favorites button.) You can add or remove assets as needed to streamline your work environment.
21 Display the Files panel	
Collapse the images folder	Click the minus sign next to the images folder.
22 Double-click **index.html**	To open the page.
Right-click the peppers image	
Choose **Add to Image Favorites**	To add this asset to the Favorites directly from the page. When you add an item to the Favorites list directly from a page, Dreamweaver does not prompt you to confirm the action.
23 Verify that the image is in the Favorite images list	

Blank pages and templates

Explanation

Dreamweaver provides several options for creating Web pages. You can create pages from scratch, or you can use layout templates. Depending on the nature of your site and your own development preferences, you might choose to start from scratch, or you might prefer to have some of the work done for you before you get started.

To create a Web page, choose File, New. This opens the New Document dialog box, which displays several options, described in the following table.

Option	Description
Blank Page	You can create a new, blank HTML page that contains only the basic document tag structure with no content. You can also create a blank page that contains "dummy" content in a preset layout that you can modify to suit your needs. Using the Blank Page category of the New Document dialog box, you can also create CSS documents, XML documents, and many other types of documents.
Blank Template	This set of options provides HTML templates, plus templates for server technologies such as ASP.NET and ColdFusion. These templates are attached to predefined CSS style sheets, which provide a layout framework that you can build on.
Page from Template	This option shows a list of your own templates from which you can create pages.
Page from Sample	This option provides several basic style sheets that you can use and modify.

Starting with a blank HTML page

To create a blank HTML page:

ACA objective 4.2a

1 Choose File, New to open the New Document dialog box. (You can also press Ctrl+N.)
2 Select Blank Page (if necessary).
3 In the Page Type list, verify that HTML is selected (at the top of the list).
4 In the Layout list, verify that <none> is selected, and then click Create.

File names and file extensions

ACA objectives 4.2b, 4.2c, 4.2d

The file name you choose for your home page is important. Home pages are usually named index.html or default.html because Web servers are typically configured to look for that file name as the Web site's *root*, or top-level file. File names cannot include special characters such as (, $, #, @ and &, and cannot contain spaces. You can use underscore characters if you want to separate words or letters.

When you save a new Web page, it's important that you name it with the appropriate file extension, such as .htm or .html. If applicable, check with your server administrator to verify the naming conventions in use in your organization. You might also need to save pages with file extensions for specific application processing, such as .asp for an Active Server Pages document or .cfm for a ColdFusion document.

Page titles

ACA objectives 4.2e, 4.2f

You should give every page a title. Titles are not the same as file names; titles appear in the title bar of the browser window and are used by some search engines to help provide accurate search results. To specify a page title, enter it in the Title box on the Document toolbar or in the Title box in the Property inspector.

Document tabs

You can have multiple documents open simultaneously and switch between them by clicking the document tabs. You can also display files as floating documents so that each one appears in its own window. To open each tabbed document in a floating window, choose Window, Cascade. To return a floating window to the standard tabbed format, click the Maximize button in the upper-right corner of the window.

Do it! ## B-2: Creating a new page

Here's how	Here's why
1 Choose **File, New...**	To open the New Document dialog box.
Verify that **Blank Page** is selected	
Verify that **HTML** and **<none>** are selected	In the Page Type list and the Layout list, respectively.
Click **Create**	To open a blank HTML page.
ACA objectives 4.2e, 4.2f 2 On the Document toolbar, edit the Title box to read **Outlander Spices: Books**	Title: Outlander Spices: Books To give the new page a title. This text will appear in the browser window's title bar.
3 Choose **File, Save**	(Or press Ctrl+S.) The Save As dialog box appears because this is a new document that hasn't been saved yet.
ACA objectives 4.2a, 4.2b Edit the File name box to read **books.html**	File name: books.html
Click **Save**	
4 Verify that books.html appears in the Files panel list	
5 Observe the document tabs	Dw File Edit View I index.html ✕ books.html ✕ You can switch between open files by clicking their tabs.
Click the **index.html** tab	To switch to the home page.
Go back to books.html	

Inserting and importing text

Explanation

You can add text to a Web page by typing in the Document window. If the text is in a separate file, you can import the text or copy and paste it into Dreamweaver.

ACA objective 4.3a

It's often helpful to use an external file as the source of your Web site text so you can distribute the file for editing and approval by other members of a development team. When the text is approved and ready, you can copy and paste it into Dreamweaver. You can import text from a text file or from a formatted document, such as a Microsoft Word document.

Importing text

ACA objective 4.10a

You can import content by dragging a file from the Files panel to the Document window. When you do this, the Insert Document dialog box prompts you to specify your import and formatting preferences, as shown in Exhibit 2-5.

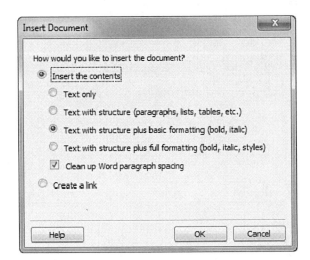

Exhibit 2-5: The Insert Document dialog box

The options in the Insert Document dialog box are described in the following table.

Option	Description
Insert the contents	Copies the file's text into the Web page.
Text only	Inserts plain text without any formatting.
Text with structure	Inserts plain text and retains structures such as paragraph breaks, lists, and tables.
Text with structure plus basic formatting	Inserts plain or structured text. If any text uses basic formatting, such as boldface or italics, Dreamweaver retains this formatting by adding HTML tags when necessary.
Text with structure plus full formatting	Inserts plain or structured text and retains all HTML tags and internal CSS styles.
Clean up Word paragraph spacing	Removes extra spacing above and below paragraphs in documents imported from Microsoft Word.
Create a link	Inserts a hyperlink to the text file (rather than inserting the text itself).

ACA objective 4.10b appears beside the "Text only" row.

Pasting text from other sources

ACA objectives 4.10a, 4.10b

Using the standard Copy and Paste commands is another way to bring content from another application into Dreamweaver. To control how Dreamweaver formats content pasted from another application, choose Edit, Paste Special. The formatting options in the Paste Special dialog box, shown in Exhibit 2-6, are the same as those in the Insert Document dialog box.

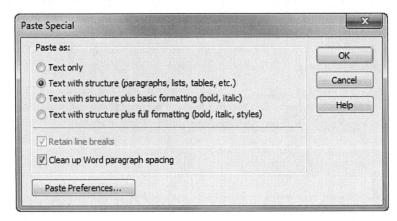

Exhibit 2-6: The Paste Special dialog box

Do it!

ACA objectives 4.10a, 4.10b

B-3: Importing text

Here's how	Here's why
1 Drag **booksinfo1.doc** from the Files panel to the Document window	The Insert Document dialog box appears. You'll import text from this Microsoft Word file and then from a simple text file.
2 Verify that **Insert the contents** is selected	
Verify that **Text with structure plus basic formatting (bold, italic)** is selected	To import the text and any basic formatting.
Verify that **Clean up Word paragraph spacing** is selected	To remove unnecessary spaces and returns and other unwanted characters from the Word document.
Click **OK**	To insert the text as specified. Notice that "Outlander Cooking!" appears in italics—the basic formatting was retained.
3 If necessary, place the insertion point as shown	⌐ew ingredients and combinati easy-to-follow instructions.⎮
Press ⎗ENTER	To start a new paragraph.
4 Drag **booksinfo2.txt** below the current text	(From the Files panel.) To add more text from another type of file. The Insert Document dialog box appears.
5 Click **OK**	To insert the text and close the Insert Document dialog box. This is a plain text file with no formatting.
6 Save the page	

Point out that this text is from a text file, not a Microsoft Word file.

Page properties

Explanation

ACA objective 5.1a

With the Page Properties dialog box, you can set basic page design options, such as the font, font size, and background color. To open the Page Properties dialog box, you can click the Page Properties button in the Property inspector, choose Modify, Page Properties, or press Ctrl+J.

When you use the Page Properties dialog box to apply styles, they will be applied to the current page only. When you want multiple pages to share the same styles, you need to use a style sheet.

Page margins

A *page margin* is the space between the content on a page and the edges of the browser window. (Margins may also exist between individual elements.) Browsers apply their own default page margins, typically between 10 and 15 pixels of space on all four sides. It's important that you set your own page margins to ensure that they are consistent in different browsers.

You can also set your page margins to zero so that some of your content, such as a navigation bar or header logo, can appear flush with the edge of the browser window. You can then apply margins to large content sections or individual elements to ensure that other content is offset from the browser window's edge and other page elements.

Background color

By default, Web pages have a white background, but you can apply any background color. To do so, select a color from the Background color box in the Page Properties dialog box. Clicking the Background color box opens a *color picker*—a palette with a set of color swatches, as shown in Exhibit 2-7. By default, the color picker displays the Web Safe Colors, a standard set of 216 colors supported consistently by various operating systems.

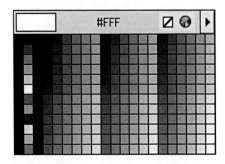

Exhibit 2-7: The color picker

Setting a default text color

Text is black by default. You can change the color of text that you select on a page, or you can set a default color for all text on a page by using the Page Properties dialog box. You might want to do this if your Web site uses a colored background that makes black text difficult to read or if you just want to establish a complementary color scheme.

Whenever you apply text colors and background colors, you should make sure that there's sufficient contrast between them to allow for easy reading. Insufficient contrast can strain the eyes and make reading difficult.

Do it!

B-4:   Setting page properties

Here's how	Here's why
1 In the Property inspector, click **Page Properties...**	To open the Page Properties dialog box. You'll set basic style attributes for the current page.
In the Category list, verify that **Appearance (CSS)** is selected	You will apply styles by using CSS (Cascading Style Sheets), instead of HTML attributes.

ACA objective 5.1a

Have students verify that #FFC appears at the top of the color picker.

2 Click the Background color box	A color picker appears. The pointer changes to an eyedropper.
Click as shown	
	(In the bottom-right corner.) To apply a pale yellow color.
3 Click the Text color box	To open the color picker.
Select a dark green color	Select the color #060 or a similar dark green
Click **Apply**	To apply the changes without closing the dialog box. The page now has a pale yellow background, and the text is dark green.
4 In the Left margin box, enter **20**	To give the page a left margin of 20 pixels.
5 In the three other margin boxes, enter **20**	To set the margin to 20 pixels on all four sides of the page.
6 Click **OK**	To apply the changes and close the Page Properties dialog box. Notice that there is now slightly more space between the text and the edges of the page.
7 Save and close all files	Press Ctrl+S or choose File, Save.

Topic C: Working with code

This topic covers the following Adobe ACA exam objectives for Dreamweaver CS5.

#	Objective
3.1b	Demonstrate knowledge of the differences between Design view, Code view, Split view, and Live view.
3.1d	Demonstrate knowledge of working with related files and the Code Navigator.
4.1b	Demonstrate knowledge of the steps for defining a new Dreamweaver site.
5.3c	Demonstrate knowledge of how to apply a paragraph style to a paragraph of text.
5.6a	Demonstrate knowledge of HTML tags.

Basic HTML

Explanation

HTML code defines the basic structure of a Web page. Even if you prefer to work in Design view, you should be familiar with basic HTML syntax.

An HTML tag tells a browser how to interpret or display the content enclosed in the tag. For example, the <h1> tag identifies a line of text as a level-one heading, and the browser renders it accordingly.

HTML tags are enclosed in angle brackets: < >. Most HTML tags consist of a beginning tag and an ending tag. The ending tag includes a forward slash (/), which tells the browser that the tag instruction has ended. For example, the following code is a snippet of text that uses the <b> tag to define bold text:

```
Outlander Spices offers only the <b>best</b> spices.
```

A Web browser would display this text as follows:

Outlander Spices offers only the **best** spices.

The following code shows the basic structure of an HTML document. Notice that some tags are nested inside other tags, and there's an ending tag for each starting tag.

```
<html>
  <head>
     <title>Document Title</title>
  </head>
  <body>
     All rendered HTML and content are inserted here.
  </body>
</html>
```

ACA objective 5.6a

The standard tags that begin an HTML document are <html>, <head>, and <body>. The <html> element is considered the *root element,* or top-level element. All other HTML tags reside within the <html> tag. It defines the document as an HTML document. HTML documents are then divided into two sections: the <head> section and the <body> section.

The <head> section contains the <title> element, which defines the document's title. This section may also contain style sheet information, meta information, scripts, and other code or resources that aren't rendered on the page.

The <body> section contains all of the content (text, images, etc.) that's rendered on the page, along with the code for it. Each tag in the <body> section performs a specific function to define the content. The following table describes a few of the most commonly used HTML tags.

Tag	Description
<div>	Defines a logical section (division) of a page.
<p>	Defines a paragraph.
<table>	Creates a table, which is composed of rows and columns.

ACA objective 5.6a

Document views

ACA objective 3.1b

As shown in Exhibit 2-8, there are three main view buttons at the top of the Document window: Code, Split, and Design. Design view is the default view. You can click the Code button to switch to Code view, for working directly with the HTML code. Click the Split button to split the document window into Code view and Design view.

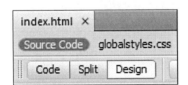

Exhibit 2-8: The buttons for Code view, Split view, and Design view

Working with code

Dreamweaver provides several tools for selecting and modifying code. In Code view, you can use the Coding toolbar and the Tag Editor to perform common tasks and edit code. In Design view, you can use the Quick Tag Editor to insert and edit code.

The Coding toolbar

When you work in Code view, the Coding toolbar is displayed vertically along the left side of the Document window. You can use the Coding toolbar to perform common coding tasks, such as indenting code, expanding and collapsing code sections, and adding and removing comments.

The Tag Editor

When you're working in Code view, you can right-click a tag and choose Edit Tag to open the Tag Editor for that tag. In the Tag Editor, you can modify tag attributes, which are sorted by category, and get more information about the tag.

Selecting tags with the tag selector

In both Code view and Design view, you can use the tag selector to select a specific element and its contents. Depending on the current selection or location of the insertion point, the tag selector shows the parent tags, all the way back to the <body> element, as shown in Exhibit 2-9. The tag selector is located in the status bar at the bottom of the Document window.

`<body> <table> <tr> <td> <div> <a>`

Exhibit 2-9: The tag selector, showing nested tags

The Quick Tag Editor

When you're working in Design view, you can add HTML tags by using the Quick Tag Editor. To insert an HTML tag, click on the page where you want to insert the tag and then press Ctrl+T. The Quick Tag Editor opens, with a prompt that reads "Insert HTML," followed by a scrollable list of HTML tags, as shown in Exhibit 2-10. Double-click an element in the list to insert it. You can then add attributes within the Quick Tag Editor, or you can press Enter. If you press Enter, the Quick Tag Editor closes and you can type at the insertion point to insert text inside the new HTML tag.

Exhibit 2-10: The Quick Tag Editor

You can also use the Quick Tag Editor to wrap a tag around a selection. Select the text, and then press Ctrl+T to open the Quick Tag Editor. The "Wrap tag:" prompt appears. Double-click an element in the list and press Enter.

The Code Navigator

ACA objective 3.1d

When you see the Code Navigator indicator, which looks like a ship's steering wheel, you can click it to see code sources relevant to the selected element, such as style sheets, templates, and script files. You can then click an item in the Code Navigator to open the code source. The insertion point is automatically placed at the spot of the selected code, so you can quickly edit specific code, rather than having to scroll through a document looking for the code you want to edit. You can hold down the Alt key and click any page element to open the Code Navigator for that element.

Selecting text in Design view

There are several ways you can select text for editing or formatting:

- Drag across the text you want to select.
- Click a word twice to select the whole word.
- Click three times anywhere in a paragraph to select that paragraph.

Do it!

C-1: Working with code and code tools

The files for this activity are in Student Data folder **Unit 2\Topic C**.

Here's how	Here's why
ACA objective 4.1b 1 Choose **Site, New Site...**	To open the Site Setup dialog box.
In the Site Name box, type **Outlander**	To name the site.
Click as shown	
	To open the Choose Root Folder dialog box.
Tell students to navigate up one level to the current topic folder. 2 In the current topic folder, open the Outlander Spices folder	You'll need to navigate up to the current topic folder.
Click **Select**	To set the root folder for this site.
Click **Save**	
3 Open **index.html**	Double-click it in the Files panel.
ACA objective 3.1b 4 Click Split	(On the Document toolbar.) To split the Document window into Code view and Design view.
5 In Design view, click an image on the page	To select it. Code view automatically highlights the code that defines the selected object.
ACA objective 3.1b 6 Click Code	To switch to Code view.
Facilitate a brief discussion of the questions that follow. *ACA objective 5.6a* 7 Locate the `<head>` tag	Scroll up, if necessary.
What's the purpose of this element?	***It contains the document's title, style sheet information, meta information, scripts, and other code or resources that aren't rendered on the page.***
8 Locate the `<body>` tag	
ACA objective 5.6a What's the purpose of this element?	***It contains all of the content (text, images, and so on) that is rendered on a page, along with the code for it.***

In the "Click as shown" step, a screenshot shows a folder icon with a "Browse for folder" tooltip.

9 Under the `<body>` tag, right-click the first **`<table>`** tag

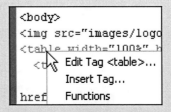

To display a shortcut menu.

Choose **Edit Tag `<table>`...**

To open the Tag Editor for the `<table>` tag. You can right-click any tag in Code view to open the Tag Editor, where you can modify attributes and get more information about the element.

Observe the options

You can modify a tag's attributes, which are grouped in separate categories.

10 Click **Tag info**, as shown

(At the bottom of the dialog box.) To open a reference window.

Briefly scroll through the reference window

You can get information about the selected tag and see usage examples.

Click **Cancel**

To close the dialog box without making any changes. The entire `<table>` tag, with all of its content, is selected, even if you cancel out of the Tag Editor.

11 Click anywhere in Code view

To deselect the `<table>` element.

12 Triple-click the **`<table>`** tag

To select the entire line of code—only the line, and not the entire block defined by the `<table>` tag.

Press and hold (SHIFT)

Click to the right of the closing `</table>` tag, as shown

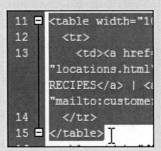

(At line 15.) To select the `<table>` element and the content it contains.

Release (SHIFT)

	13 On the Coding toolbar, click ⟨⟩	(The Collapse Full Tag button.) To collapse everything between the opening and closing `<table>` tags. You might find it helpful to collapse certain code blocks if you want to focus on other areas of code.
| | Click as shown | ```
14   <body>
15   <img src="ima
16 ⊓ <table ...
21   <table width=
22     <tr>
``` |
		To expand the selection.
ACA objective 3.1b	14 Click [Design]	To switch to Design view. Notice that the table that contains the navigation bar is selected.
	15 Click anywhere in the first paragraph	To place the insertion point.
	In the tag selector, click **\<p>**, as shown	`<body> <table> <tr> <td> <table> <tr> <td> <p>` **PROPERTIES**
		The paragraph is selected on the page. Use the tag selector when you want to select an element and its content.
	What does a **\<p>** tag do?	***A \<p> tag defines a paragraph of text.***
	16 Switch to Code view	The paragraph tags are selected in addition to the content they contain. Typing over this selection will replace the paragraph tags and the content.
	Switch to Design view	
Be sure that students have switched back to Design view.	17 Triple-click the paragraph shown	this Web site. We are dedicated to providing spices exceptional quality and variety. Discover a whole new world of flavor: look for an Outlander Spices kiosk in a store near you!
		To select the whole paragraph.
	Switch to Code view	Only the text content is selected, not the paragraph tags that contain it.
	Switch to Design view	
	18 Press (CTRL) + (T)	To open the Quick Tag Editor. You can use this tool to insert HTML tags in Design view.
ACA objectives 5.6a, 5.3c	19 In the list of tags, double-click **b** and then press (↵ ENTER)	To wrap the selected text inside a `<b>` tag, which makes the text bold.
	Click anywhere on the page	To deselect the paragraph.
```

ACA objective 3.1d

Students can point to body to see the margin styles they applied earlier.

20	Click anywhere in the first paragraph	After a moment, the Code Navigator indicator appears. It looks like a ship's steering wheel.
	After a moment, click	To open the Code Navigator. It shows that the only code affecting this paragraph is in the style sheet file globalstyles.css. There is no code directly applied to this paragraph.
	Select **Disable**	To turn off the Code Navigator indicator.
	Click away from the Code Navigator	To close it. You can always Alt+click an element to open the Code Navigator.
21	Save the page	

Special characters

Explanation

Some characters that you might need in your content, such as the copyright symbol (©) or language-specific characters like the umlaut (ü), are not included on a computer keyboard. You can insert these special characters in Code view by entering their corresponding *character entities*, which are HTML codes that begin with an ampersand (&) and end with a semicolon. The following table lists some common examples.

Character	Symbol	HTML code
Copyright	©	`&copy;`
Registered trademark	®	`&reg;`
Degree	°	`&deg;`

The codes required for these special characters aren't always intuitive or easy to remember, so Dreamweaver provides a list to choose from. To insert a special character:

1 In Code view, place the insertion point where you want the special character to appear.
2 Type & (ampersand). A list of special characters appears.
3 Scroll through the list to find the desired character. The HTML code for the character appears in the right column in black, and the character appears in the left column in blue.
4 Select a character from the list.

You can also insert special characters in Design view. Place the insertion point where you want to insert the character and choose Insert, HTML, Special Characters, and then choose an option from the list.

Non-breaking spaces

When you're working in Design view, you can't insert more than one standard space between words by using the Spacebar. If you want to insert more than one space, choose Insert, HTML, Special Characters, Non-Breaking Space (or press Ctrl+Shift+Space). This adds a single space without forcing a line break. You can also switch to Code view and manually enter the non-breaking space character, which is ` `.

Do it!

C-2: Inserting special characters and spaces

Here's how	Here's why
1 Switch to Code view	You'll add a copyright symbol to the page footer.
Scroll to the bottom of the page	You'll replace the word "Copyright" with the copyright symbol.
Double-click **Copyright**	ter">Copyright Outlander
	To select it. (You can also drag to select it.)
2 Type **&**	A list appears, showing a variety of special characters.
3 Type **co**	The copyright symbol is selected in the list. (You could also scroll through the list to find the character you're looking for.)
4 Press (↵ ENTER)	To insert the code for the copyright symbol.
5 Switch to Design view	To verify that the text has been replaced with the copyright symbol.
Switch to Code view	
6 Place the insertion point as shown	Spices. |All rights
	You'll insert spaces after the copyright notice.
Press (SPACEBAR) four times	To insert four spaces in the HTML code.
Switch to Design view	The ordinary spaces entered in the HTML code don't have any effect.
7 Switch to Code view and delete the four spaces	(Press Backspace four times.) You'll insert non-breaking spaces instead.
8 Type **&**	To display the list of special characters.
Type **nb**	To select nbsp; from the list.
Press (↵ ENTER)	To insert a non-breaking space.
9 Insert three more non-breaking spaces, as shown	All
10 Switch to Design view	The four non-breaking spaces create additional space between the two copyright statements.
11 Save your changes	

Point out that students need to type only a partial entry. The list will jump to the desired character.

TIPS ✓ *Tell students that they can also use Copy and Paste.*

Finding and replacing content and code

If you need to convert multiple instances of a particular word, phrase, or code, you can use the Find and Replace dialog box. Using Find and Replace can help you save time and prevent omissions. You can find and replace content and code within a single document, a selection, a specific folder, or an entire site.

To find and replace content or code:

1 Choose Edit, Find and Replace (or press Ctrl + F) to open the Find and Replace dialog box.

2 From the Search list, select an option, depending on what you need to find and replace.

3 In the Find box, enter the text or code you want to find.

4 In the Replace box, enter the replacement text or code.

5 Click Find Next. The first instance of the item you're looking for is selected (if it exists).

6 Click Replace to replace the selection with the replacement text or code.

7 Click Find Next to continue, click Replace All to replace all instances of the item, or click Close to close the dialog box.

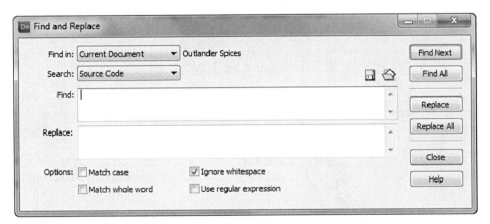

Exhibit 2-11: The Find and Replace dialog box

If you select Source Code from the Search list, Dreamweaver switches to Code view when you initiate the search. You can also select the Text (Advanced) option, which allows you to focus your search on tags that are inside (or *not* inside) other HTML tags that you specify. Finally, you can select Specific Tag to search for and replace tags that contain specific attributes or attribute values.

Do it!

C-3: Finding and replacing content and code

Here's how	Here's why
1 Switch to Code view	
2 Choose **Edit, Find and Replace...**	To open the Find and Replace dialog box. You'll replace the text "Copyright" with the code for the copyright symbol in every other page in the site.
From the Find in list, select **Entire Current Local Site**	
In the Search list, verify that **Source Code** is selected	
3 In the Find box, type **Copyright**	
In the Replace box, type **©**	
4 Click **Find Next**	The aboutus.html page opens with the text "Copyright" selected.
Move the dialog box so that you can see the selection on the page	If necessary.
Click **Replace**	To replace the text with the character entity for the copyright symbol. The locations.html page opens with the search text selected.
5 Click **Replace All**	A dialog box opens, warning that this command cannot be undone in documents that are not open.
Click **Yes**	To replace all instances of the word "Copyright" with the code for the copyright symbol in every document in the site.
6 Observe the Search panel	(At the bottom of the application window.) The Search tab displays a list of the replacements made in documents that are not open.
Right-click the **Search** tab	
Choose **Close Tab Group**	
7 Switch to Design view	
Scroll down to the bottom of the active page	(If necessary.) The copyright statement now begins with the copyright symbol.

TIPS Students can also press Ctrl+F.

Point out that any Find and Replace command that deals with code must be issued in Code view.

Point out that you can replace one instance at a time to verify each one, or use Replace All to make all replacements in one step.

Point out the results message at the bottom of the dialog box.

8 Choose **File**, **Close All**	To close all open documents. A dialog box prompts you to save before closing.
Click **Yes** until all files are closed	To update each file.

Unit summary: Web sites and pages

Topic A   In this topic, you learned about some common planning and **organizational tools** and methods. You learned about flowcharts, storyboards, and wireframes, which you can use to plan your site before you start building it. You also learned about some **basic design principles**, including the importance of contrast, layout consistency, and readability.

Topic B   In this topic, you learned how to **define a local site**, and use the Files panel and Assets panel to manage your site files and folders. You also learned how to create and save a page, give a page a title, **import text** from other sources, and set basic **page properties**, including page margins, text color, and background color.

Topic C   In this topic, you learned how to use the **code tools** and you learned basic HTML syntax. You also learned how to **select text** on a page and select code in Code view. You used the **Tag Editor** to modify HTML elements, and you used the Quick Tag Editor to insert HTML tags in Design view. You also inserted **special characters** and non-breaking spaces. Finally, you used the **Find and Replace** tool to replace content and code.

Independent practice activity

In this activity, you'll define a Web site, create a page, and add text to it. Then you'll set page margins and save the page.

The files for this activity are in Student Data folder **Unit 2\Unit summary**.

1 Open the Site Setup dialog box and enter **Outlander Practice** as the site name.

2 Browse to the Unit summary folder and select the Outlander Spices folder.

3 In the Site Setup dialog box, click Save.

4 Create a new, blank page and title it **Outlander Spices: Videos**.

5 Save the page as **videos.html**.

6 Import the text from videos.doc into the new videos.html page.

7 Set the left page margin to **30**, and the top page margin to **15**. (*Hint:* In the Property inspector, click Page Properties.)

8 Give the page a light background color of your choice.

9 Use the Quick Tag Editor to wrap the first block of text in a paragraph tag. (*Hint:* Select the paragraph first.)

10 Save and close videos.html.

11 From the Files panel, open index.html. Scroll to the bottom of the page.

12 Use the Find and Replace dialog box to replace all instances of the copyright symbol with **All Contents ©**, as shown in Exhibit 2-12. (*Hint:* From the Find in list, select Entire Current Local Site. From the Search list, select Source Code.)

13 Save and close all open files.

All contents © Outlander Spices. All rights reserved.

Exhibit 2-12: The modified copyright statement.

Review questions

1 _____ were used by early creators of animated movies to plan and visualize a story before beginning the actual drawing for the film.

   A Folios

   B Dailies

   c Storyboards

   D Flipbooks

2 The Assets panel displays which of the following? [Choose all that apply.]

   A The images in the Web site

   B The folders in the Web site

   c The colors in use in the Web site

   D The HTML files that make up the Web site

   E The script files in the Web site

3 How can you add a title to a page?

   A Double-click the page and enter the title in the Page Title dialog box.

   B Choose Insert, Page Title, and enter the title in the Page Title dialog box.

   C Enter the title in the Page Title box in the Property inspector.

   D Enter the title in the Title box on the Document toolbar.

4 How can you open the Page Properties dialog box? [Choose all that apply.]

   A Double-click the page.

   B In the Property inspector, click the Page Properties button.

   C Ctrl+click the page.

   D Choose Modify, Page Properties.

5 What's the keyboard shortcut to open the Find and Replace dialog box?

   A Ctrl + R

   B Ctrl + F

   C Alt + R

   D Alt + F

6 How can you view the code for a document? [Choose all that apply.]

   A Press F1.

   B Click the Code button at the top of the Document window.

   C Press F5.

   D Click the Split button at the top of the Document window.

7 You're displaying a page in Design view. How can you show the Coding toolbar?

   A Switch to Code view.

   B Choose View, Toolbars, Coding.

   C Choose Window, Code Inspector.

   D Choose View, Code View Options, Coding.

8 In Code view, how can you collapse a selected tag? [Choose all that apply.]

   A Choose Modify, Collapse Full Tag.

   B On the Coding toolbar, click the Collapse Full Tag button.

   C Double-click the tag.

   D To the left of the tag, click the small minus sign (–) .

9 True or false? To add HTML tags to a page, you need to work in Code view.

   False. You can also add HTML tags in Design view by using the Quick Tag Editor.

10 In Design view, how can you select an entire paragraph, but not its containing HTML tag? [Choose all that apply.]

   A Use the tag selector.

   B Drag to select the paragraph.

   C Triple-click anywhere inside the paragraph.

   D Double-click anywhere inside the paragraph.

11 What's the keyboard shortcut for opening the Quick Tag Editor?

   A Ctrl+Q

   B Shift+T

   C Ctrl+T

   D Ctrl+E

Unit 3

Structure and style

Unit time: 60 minutes

Complete this unit, and you'll know how to:

A Define a basic page structure, and create and modify lists.

B Create CSS style sheets, apply styles to text, and create and apply class styles.

Topic A: Structure

This topic covers the following Adobe ACA exam objectives for Dreamweaver CS5.

#	Objective
2.1b	Identify techniques used to maintain consistency.
2.1e	Identify features used to maintain page structure and content hierarchy.
4.3b	Demonstrate knowledge of the effect of pressing the Enter key and pressing Shift + Enter when typing text in Design view.
5.3d	Demonstrate knowledge of how to indent text to set off a block quotation.
5.3f	Demonstrate knowledge of ordered, unordered, and definition lists.
5.3g	Demonstrate knowledge of how to create unordered and ordered lists and how to set properties for a list by using the List Item button in the Property inspector.
5.3h	Demonstrate knowledge of how to create definition lists.
5.6a	Demonstrate knowledge of HTML tags.

Document structure

Explanation

Headings, paragraphs, and other structural elements allow you to organize a Web page into a logical hierarchy, which can make your pages more searchable, easier to read, and easier for other developers to modify. A well-designed page structure can also make it easier to design and arrange your page content and make your content accessible to users with alternative browsing devices.

Good authoring habits

There are many ways to build a Web page, but it's important that you use HTML tags in their proper context to define a meaningful page structure. For example, if you want to create a heading for a page or a section, you should define the text as a heading and not simply change the appearance of the text to *resemble* a heading. The heading level you choose should logically reflect the nature of the content.

So, for a heading that serves as the top-level heading on a page, you should define it as Heading 1. To do so, select the text, and in the Property inspector, select Heading 1 from the Format list. In the code, the text will be defined by the `<h1>` tag. You can also manually enclose the text in an `<h1>` tag if you prefer to work in Code view.

ACA objectives 2.1b, 2.1e

Creating meaningful and logical document structures establishes consistency on your pages, saves you time and effort when you later update your pages, and allows your pages to be indexed by search engines more efficiently. Focusing on establishing a meaningful document structure typically results in an efficient document with a small file size, or "page weight," especially when all style-related information is contained in an external style sheet. The smaller the file size, the faster the page will load.

Headings and paragraphs

ACA objective 5.6a

When you're creating a document that requires multiple headings and subheadings, think of it as a traditional outline. HTML includes six headings that you can use to structure your documents—Heading 1 through Heading 6. The tags for these headings are <h1> through <h6>. Browsers apply their own default formatting to these headings, which you can change using a style sheet.

Headings are bold by default, and they use different font sizes. The <h1> tag applies the largest default font size, and the <h6> tag applies the smallest default font size. For example, if you're creating a page intended to deliver company news, an effective structure might look something like this:

```
<h1>Company News</h1>
<p>First paragraph of Company News...</p>
<p>Second paragraph of Company News...</p>
<h2>Subheading of Company News</h2>
<p>First paragraph of subtopic...</p>
```

To define a block of text as a paragraph, click inside the text block and select Paragraph from the Format list in the Property inspector. If you need to divide a block of text into separate paragraphs, simply place the insertion point where you want to begin a new paragraph and press Enter.

Block quotes

ACA objective 5.3d

If you have a line or block of text that's a quotation, you can define it as such to distinguish it from other text. First click inside the text (or select the text) and then click the Blockquote button in the Property inspector. A <blockquote> tag is inserted to define the text. By default, block quotes are indented on both sides.

Do it!

A-1: Defining headings and paragraphs

The files for this activity are in Student Data folder **Unit 3\Topic A**.

Here's how	Here's why
1 Choose **Site, New Site...**	To open the Site Setup dialog box.
2 In the Site Name box, type **Outlander Structure**	To name the site.
3 Browse to the current topic folder	Many topics in this course have an Outlander Spices folder, so be sure to choose the current unit and topic folder.
Open the Outlander Spices folder, click **Select**, and click **Save**	To set the root folder for this site and create the site.
4 Open aboutus.html	From the Files panel.
Click **About us**	(At the top of the page.) To place the insertion point in this line. This text is defined by a paragraph tag.
5 In the Property inspector, from the Format list, select **Heading 1**	To convert the text to a level-one heading. Browsers render level-one headings a certain way by default, but you can change the formatting with a style sheet.
6 In Code view, observe the heading code	The text is now enclosed in `<h1>` tags to define it as a top-level heading.
Switch to Design view	
7 Convert **About our spices** to a level-two heading	(Click the text and select Heading 2 from the Format list in the Property inspector.) This heading is not quite as large as Heading 1.
8 Convert the **Spice blends...** line to a level-two heading	Scroll down, if necessary.
9 Convert **Expansion project** to a level-two heading	
10 Switch to Code view	
Observe the first block of text	The text block is not defined by any HTML tag. You'll define it as a paragraph.
Switch to Design view	
11 Click anywhere inside the first text block	To place the insertion point.
Observe the Format list in the Property inspector	The Format list reads "None" because this text is not defined by any HTML element.

Students will need to define a new site to start each new topic.

Again, be sure students navigate to the current topic folder in the current unit folder.

Consider having students switch to Code view briefly to see that the text is currently defined as a paragraph. Then have them switch back.

ACA objective 2.1e

ACA objective 5.6a

Point out that it won't look like any change has occurred until students view the code.	12 From the Format list, select **Paragraph**	Nothing appears to happen, but the text block is now defined as a paragraph.
ACA objective 5.6a	Switch to Code view	Note that the text is now contained in a `<p>` tag. It's important that you always put your text content inside a paragraph tag or another HTML tag, depending on the purpose of the content.
	Switch to Design view	
	13 Click before the second-to last sentence, as shown	Outlander Spices ope provide the highest qu throughout the USA a United States, and we few years. |Outlander Oregon, and we have
		(In that same paragraph.) To place the insertion point.
	Press ↵ ENTER	To create a new paragraph.
ACA objective 4.3b	Switch to Code view	You created a separate paragraph simply by pressing the Enter key.
	14 Switch back to Design view	
	Define the remaining text blocks as paragraphs	
	15 Click as shown	|All contents © Outlander
		To place the insertion point.
	Press SHIFT + ↵ ENTER	To move the text down one line.
ACA objective 4.3b	Switch to Code view and observe the result	In Design view, pressing Shift+Enter does not create a new paragraph but instead inserts a line break, the ` ` tag. (The `<p>` tag was already there.) Line breaks force text down one line within the paragraph.
	16 Switch to Design view	
	17 Click the paragraph under "Expansion Project"	You'll create a block quote.
ACA objective 5.3d	Click 🔳	(The Blockquote button is in the Property inspector.) To define the text as a block quote. By default, block quotes are indented on both sides.
	18 Save and close the page	

Lists

Explanation

*ACA objectives 2.1e,
5.6a*

You can create unordered, ordered, and definition lists. (Unordered lists are also called *bulleted lists*, and ordered lists are also called *numbered lists*.) In an unordered list, a bullet (black circle), square, or custom icon precedes each list item. By default, an unordered list uses black bullets, as shown in Exhibit 3-1. Use an unordered list when the sequence of the list items is not important or relevant. The HTML tag `<ul>` starts an unordered list, and each list item is defined by an `<li>` tag.

ACA objective 5.3f

Our most popular spices include:

- Bay leaf
- Cinnamon
- Coriander
- Nutmeg
- Turmeric

Exhibit 3-1: An unordered list

ACA objective 5.6a

In an ordered list, a number or letter indicates each item's order in the list, as shown in Exhibit 3-2. By default, ordered lists are numbered 1, 2, 3, and so on. You can also choose Alphabet Large (A, B, C), Alphabet Small (a, b, c), Roman Large (I, II, III), or Roman Small (i, ii, iii). Use an ordered list when the sequence of items is important.

The `<ol>` tag starts an ordered list, and each list item is defined by an `<li>` tag.

Directions:

1. Whisk the yogurt with the paste. Mix well.
2. Heat the oil, reduce the heat, and then add onions, ginger and garlic.
3. Add the potatoes and fry until golden brown.
4. Add the yogurt paste.
5. Cook for 5 minutes.
6. Add ¾ cup of warm water. Bring to a boil and reduce heat.
7. Cook until the potatoes are tender and the gravy is thick.

Exhibit 3-2: An ordered list

You can also create a definition list, which doesn't use bullets or numbers. A definition list is used for terms and their definitions and is often used in glossaries, "frequently asked questions" pages (FAQs), and similar contexts. As shown in Exhibit 3-3, each definition is indented beneath its term. This indentation is the only default formatting that browsers apply to a definition list. You might consider making the definition terms bold to distinguish them from the definition text.

Cinnamon
    Cinnamon is one of our most popular spices, due to its sweet flavor and prominent role in baked goods and candies. Cinnamon is also wonderful in stews and sauces.
Nutmeg
    Nutmeg comes from the seed of a tropical tree. It has a sweet, rich and aromatic flavor that complements meats, vegetables, tomato sauces, and baked goods.

Exhibit 3-3: A definition list

The <dl> tag starts a definition list. Each term is wrapped in a <dt> tag and definition text is wrapped in a <dd> tag, which stands for definition description.

Creating a list

ACA objectives 5.3g, 5.3h

To create a list, you can select paragraphs of text and convert them to list items by clicking the Unordered List button or the Ordered List button in the Property inspector. You can also choose Format, List and then choose Unordered List, Ordered List, or Definition List. Each selection starts a new list. You can then begin typing, and when you press the Enter key, a new numbered or bulleted list item will appear. To complete the list, press Enter twice.

After you create a list, you can change the list type or style if necessary. Click any list item and then click List Item in the Property inspector. This opens the List Properties dialog box. Select the desired list type and style, and then click OK.

Sub-lists

ACA objective 2.1e

A *sub-list*, also called a *nested list,* is a list inside another list. For example, a step in a list of instructions might require its own list of sub-steps. To make a sub-list, select the content that you want to turn into a nested list and click the Indent button in the Property inspector. Indenting a list item also changes its default bullet style, which helps to establish the hierarchical structure of the list.

A-2:   Creating lists

Here's how	Here's why
1 Open recipes.html	(Double-click the file in the Files panel.) You'll convert ordinary text to ordered and unordered lists.

2   Select all paragraphs between the "Ingredients" and "Directions" subheadings, as shown

Potatoes, washed and quartered: 2 ½ cups

Oil: ½ cup

Onions chopped: ½ cup

Yogurt: ½ cup

Dry roast and grind to a paste with a little water:

Almonds, blanched peeled and sliced: 3 tbsp

Outlander Spices Cinnamon powder: 1 ½ tsp

Outlander Spices Nutmeg powder: 1 ½ tsp

Outlander Spices Coriander powder: 1 ½ tsp

Outlander Spices Red chili powder: 3 tsp

Garlic paste: 2 tsp

Ginger paste: 2 tsp

You'll convert these paragraphs to a single unordered list.

3   In the Property inspector, click [≡]

(The Unordered List button.) To format the selected text as an unordered list.

Click anywhere on the page

Ingredients

- Potatoes, washed and quartered: 2 ½ cups
- Oil: ½ cup
- Onions chopped: ½ cup
- Yogurt: ½ cup
- **Dry roast and grind to a paste with a little water:**
- Almonds, blanched peeled and sliced: 3 tbsp
- Outlander Spices Cinnamon powder: 1 ½ tsp
- Outlander Spices Nutmeg powder: 1 ½ tsp
- Outlander Spices Coriander powder: 1 ½ tsp
- Outlander Spices Red chili powder: 3 tsp
- Garlic paste: 2 tsp
- Ginger paste: 2 tsp

To deselect the text. The paragraphs were converted to items in an unordered list, which is a more appropriate structure for this content.

4 Switch to Code view

ACA objective 5.6a

Observe the code for the unordered list

Each item in the list is defined by the `<li>` tag, and all the list items are nested inside the `<ul>` tag, the unordered list tag.

Switch to Design view

Again, because this is paragraph formatting, students can drag from anywhere in the first paragraph to anywhere in the last one.

5 Select the paragraphs under "Directions," as shown

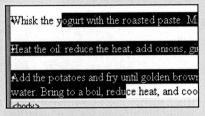

You'll convert these paragraphs into an ordered list.

Point out that each paragraph becomes a separate list item.

6 In the Property inspector, click ⁞☰

(The Ordered List button.) To convert the text to an ordered list.

Deselect the text

> ## Directions:
>
> 1. Whisk the yogurt with the roa
> 2. Heat the oil: reduce the heat,
> 3. Add the potatoes and fry unti
>   heat, and cook until the potat

(Click anywhere on the page.) To view the results. The text is now an ordered list with three sequential steps.

7 Select all list items from **Almonds** to **Red chili powder**, as shown

> - **Dry roast and grind to a paste**
>   **with a little water:**
> - Almonds, blanched peeled and sliced: 3 tbsp
> - Outlander Spices Cinnamon powder: 1 ½ tsp
> - Outlander Spices Nutmeg powder: 1 ½ tsp
> - Outlander Spices Coriander powder: 1 ½ tsp
> - Outlander Spices Red chili powder: 3 tsp
> - Garlic paste: 2 tsp
> - Ginger paste: 2 tsp

(In the first list.) You'll indent these list items to create a nested list.

ACA objective 2.1e

8 In the Property inspector, click ±☰

(The Text Indent button.) To indent this part of the list, creating a sub-list or "nested" list. The items are indented and have a different default bullet style. You can change the bullet type for a list by using CSS.

	9 Choose **Format**, **List**, **Properties...**	To open the List Properties dialog box.
	From the Style list, select **Square**	To change the bullets for the nested list to squares.
	Click **OK** and deselect the text	To apply the new bullet style to the selected items.
	10 Save and close recipes.html	
	11 Create a new, blank HTML page	Choose File, New; verify that Blank Page, HTML, and <none> are selected; and click Create.
ACA objective 5.3g	12 Choose **Format**, **List**, **Ordered List**	To create an ordered list. The number 1 is displayed on the page.
	Type some text and press `↵ ENTER`	The number 2 is displayed as the next list item.
	Type some text and press `↵ ENTER`	To create a third list item.
	Type some text and press `↵ ENTER` two times	To end the list.
	13 Click any of the list items	To place the insertion point.
ACA objective 5.3h	In the Property inspector, click **List Item...**	To open the List Properties dialog box.
	From the Style list, select **Alphabet Small (a,b,c...)**	
	Click **OK**	To format the ordered list in alphabetical order using lowercase letters.
	14 Close the file without saving it	

Topic B: Cascading Style Sheets

This topic covers the following Adobe ACA exam objectives for Dreamweaver CS5.

#	Objective
2.1b	Identify techniques used to maintain consistency.
2.1d	Identify benefits of using CSS styles.
2.1h	Demonstrate knowledge of CSS best practices.
5.1b	Demonstrate knowledge of how to set or modify global page properties and global CSS styles, including those for text, links, and backgrounds.
5.2g	Demonstrate knowledge of how to use external style sheets.
5.2h	Demonstrate knowledge of how to create CSS rules in the Property inspector.
5.3a	Demonstrate knowledge of fonts, including what viewers see if they do not have the selected font installed or if "Default Font" is selected as the font type.
5.3b	Demonstrate knowledge of how to change the font, font size, and color.
5.8a	Demonstrate knowledge of how to create inline styles and external style sheets.
5.8c	Demonstrate knowledge of the advantages of using CSS for design.
5.8e	Demonstrate knowledge of how to use different selector types, such as descendent selectors, classes, tag selectors, pseudo class selectors, and group selectors.
6.1c	Demonstrate knowledge of how to preview a Web page in a browser.
6.5g	Demonstrate knowledge of using the Related Files toolbar.

Introduction to CSS

Explanation

Cascading Style Sheets (CSS) is the standard style language for the Web. Using CSS rules, you can fully control the design and layout of your pages. For example, you can control the fonts, margins, spacing, colors, and borders that produce your site's look and feel. What makes CSS especially powerful is that you can link multiple pages to a style sheet, and therefore update all of your pages by changing the style rules in one file.

Control, efficiency, and consistency

ACA objectives 2.1b, 2.1d, 5.8c

Using a CSS style sheet to define a site means that you can focus on content and structure in your documents, without using unnecessary formatting attributes that were typical of old HTML development techniques. Style sheets mean zero redundancy; all of your site's style-related information is stored in a single location instead of being repeated on each page. This leads to faster, simpler design updates and cleaner, more efficient pages that load quickly and consistently.

Internal and external style sheets

You can define and apply styles for HTML elements by using external or internal style sheets, or both.

ACA objectives 2.1h, 5.1b

- **External style sheet** — A collection of style rules defined in a text file saved with a .css extension. You link your Web pages to the style sheet. Use external style sheets whenever you want the styles to be global—that is, when you want them to apply to multiple pages in a site. When you change a style in an external style sheet, the change is reflected in every page linked to that style sheet.

- **Internal style sheet** — A collection of style rules defined in the <head> section of an HTML document. Internal styles (also called *embedded styles*) apply only to the page in which they're defined. Use an internal style sheet when you need a style for only a single page or when you want to override a style in an external style sheet.

ACA objective 5.8a

Inline styles are another type of CSS style; they apply formatting directly to a single instance of an element. To create an inline style, you use the style attribute of any rendered HTML tag in conjunction with CSS properties. However, inline styles are a discouraged method because the style information is not kept separate from the HTML code, which eliminates one of the key benefits of using style sheets—the ability to update styles from a central location while keeping the HTML free of unnecessary clutter.

Selector types and their syntax

Style sheet rules have the following syntax:

```
selector { property: value; }
```

The *selector* defines what page element the style applies to. There are many types of selectors you can use. The most commonly used selector types are described in the following table.

Tell students that although it's good to know the basic syntax of CSS, Dreamweaver makes it easy to apply CSS styles without having to worry about the particulars of syntax.

ACA objective 5.8e

Selector	Description
Tag selectors	Also called element selectors or element styles, these style rules define the formatting of individual HTML tags. An element style overrides the default formatting for that HTML element. The syntax to define an element style is: `tag { property: value; }` For example, if you want paragraphs to appear bold, write: `p { font-weight: bold; }`
Class selectors	Class selectors allow you to give elements names that are meaningful to you. For example, you can create a class of the `<p>` element named "important" that applies bold, red text. Any paragraphs that are given that class name will appear with those styles. You can apply class styles to multiple elements on a page. The syntax for a class style is: `.className { property: value; }` Class names begin with a period. For example, to manually create the rule mentioned above, you'd write: `.important { font-weight: bold; color: red; }` A semicolon separates each style property. A style rule can contain any number of properties.
ID selectors	ID selectors also allow you to create and name your own elements. However, while a class style can be applied to multiple elements in a page, an ID style can be applied only once per document. ID styles are particularly useful for defining major content sections. The syntax for an ID style is: `#IDname { property: value; }` IDs begin with the pound sign (#). For example: `#footer { font-size: 10px; color: gray; }`

More advanced selector types include pseudo-class selectors and contextual or "descendent" selectors. Pseudo-class selectors are used to style hyperlinks in their various user-defined states, while descendent selectors target elements that exist in a particular context. For example, you can apply styles to only those paragraphs that are inside a Div tag with the ID name "content".

Do it!

B-1: Discussing style sheets and selectors

Questions and answers

Facilitate a brief discussion for each question.

1 What's a style sheet?

A style sheet is a set of rules used to control the appearance of a page or multiple pages. For example, the rules in a style sheet can control layout, margins, spacing, colors, and fonts.

2 What are the two main types of style sheets?

External and internal style sheets.

- *An external style sheet is a text file that's saved with a .css extension. The file contains CSS rules that define the appearance of multiple pages.*

- *An internal style sheet is embedded inside the <head> section of an individual Web page and influences only the elements on that page.*

ACA objectives 2.1b, 2.1d, 5.8c

3 What are the advantages of using an external style sheet?

Answers may vary. You can link multiple Web pages to an external style sheet to control the appearance of those pages from a single source. Any rule changes you make in the style sheet affect all pages that are linked to it. This feature helps to ensure that the appearance of all your site pages remains consistent. It also makes Web pages cleaner and more efficient, and it decreases the amount of work needed to change a site's design.

ACA objective 2.1h

4 When might you want to use an internal style sheet?

Answers may vary. Use an internal style sheet when a style is needed only on a particular page or when you want to override a global style on a particular page.

ACA objective 2.1d

5 How can using external style sheets help reduce the size of your HTML files?

Using external style sheets to control your site's design allows you to create clean, elegant HTML documents that contain only structure and content, instead of older, deprecated HTML attributes and methods. This results in much smaller HTML files, which load quickly and can be indexed by search engines more efficiently.

6 Name three selector types that you can define in a style sheet.

Tag selectors (or element selectors), class selectors, and ID selectors.

7 If you want the text of *all* level-one headings in your site to be blue, what type of selector should you use?

An element selector; in this case, the selector would be h1.

8 Describe a scenario in which you'd want to use a class selector.

Answers may vary. You might want to create a special kind of paragraph called "note" that you use frequently to define special information. You might want the styles for this type of paragraph to stand out more than other paragraphs.

9 Describe a scenario in which you'd want to use an ID selector.

Answers may vary. You might want to structure your page into major content sections, such as "content," "navigation," and "footer," all of which appear only once on each page.

Creating external style sheets

Explanation

ACA objectives 5.2g, 5.8a

To create a new, blank external style sheet:

1 Choose File, New to open the New Document dialog box.
2 Select Blank Page (if necessary).
3 From the Page Type list, select CSS.
4 Click Create.
5 Save the file and name it with a .css extension. (Save it in a folder dedicated to style sheets, inside your site folder.)

Creating CSS rules manually

When you create a style sheet, it opens in Code view. You can begin entering CSS rules manually, or you can create them by using the CSS Styles panel. To create a rule manually, type it on a new line. For example, to create a rule that gives all level-one headings a font size of 24 pixels, you would write:

```
h1 {font-size: 24px;}
```

As mentioned earlier, the element to the left of the braces is the *selector*—the element that will be styled. The styles (one or more properties and their values) must be inside the braces. In this example, the property is `font-size`, which is followed by a colon. After this comes the property's value, in this case, `24px`.

The semicolon is used to separate one style from the next. If a rule has only one style declaration, you don't need a semicolon, but it's a good idea to place one there anyway, in case you decide to add more properties to the rule.

Using the CSS Styles panel

You can modify CSS styles directly in a style sheet, or you can use the CSS Styles panel to view, create, edit, and delete rules and attach the style sheet to your Web site's pages. To open the CSS Styles panel, choose Window, CSS Styles.

Exhibit 3-4: The CSS Styles panel, showing one style rule in globalstyles.css

To link a Web page to an external style sheet:

1 Open the Web page.
2 At the bottom of the CSS Styles panel, click the Attach Style Sheet button (the chain-link icon). The Attach External Style Sheet dialog box opens.
3 Click Browse to open the Select Style Sheet File dialog box.
4 Navigate to and select the .css file you want to use.
5 Click OK to close the Select Style Sheet File dialog box.
6 Click OK to attach the file and close the Attach External Style Sheet dialog box.

The Related Files toolbar

ACA objective 6.5g

Above the document view buttons is the Related Files toolbar, which lists all of the files to which the current page is linked. The example in Exhibit 2-8 shows only one related file, the external style sheet globalstyles.css. (The Source Code button refers to the code of the current document.) You can click any file name on the Related Files toolbar to open that file for editing.

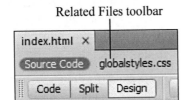

Exhibit 3-5: The Related Files toolbar

Hexadecimal color values

When you point to a color swatch, a three- or six-digit hexadecimal code for the color appears at the top of the color picker. Computer monitors use combinations of red, green, and blue to create the colors you see, and the hexadecimal scheme specifies combinations of those colors: the first two characters represent the intensity of red, the next two of green, and the last two of blue.

Hexadecimal notation uses the scale 0123456789ABCDEF, with 0 (zero) representing almost no color and F representing 15 times the intensity of 0. Hexadecimal values always start with the pound sign (#). The code #000000 (the lowest level of red, green, and blue) represents black, while #FFFFFF (the fullest intensity of red, green, and blue) represents white. To create yellow, you would add red and green, but no blue, so the hex code would be #FFFF00.

Hexadecimal codes that consist of only three values, such as #FFF or #3BA, are shortcuts for value pairs. The full values would be #FFFFFF and #33BBAA, respectively. Color values that do not consist of three matching pairs, such as #4BC9AE, cannot be reduced in this way.

Do it!

B-2:   Creating and attaching an external style sheet

The files for this activity are in Student Data folder **Unit 3\Topic B**.

Here's how	Here's why
Explain that students are only defining a new site again as a requirement of this course. 1 Choose **Site**, **New Site...**	To open the Site Setup dialog box.
2 In the Site Name box, type **Outlander CSS**	To name the site.
3 Browse to the current topic folder	
Open the Outlander Spices folder, click **Select**, and click **Save**	To set the root folder for this site and create the site.
4 Choose **File**, **New...**	To open the New Document dialog box.
Verify that **Blank Page** is selected	You'll create a new, blank style sheet.
From the Page Type list, select **CSS**	
Click **Create**	An untitled style sheet file opens in Code view.
5 Click in line 4	
Type **body {**	A list of CSS properties appears.
In the list, double-click **background-color**	A list of value options appears.
Double-click **Color...**	A color palette appears and the pointer changes to an eyedropper.
Have students verify that #FFC appears at the top of the palette. 6 Click the pale yellow color shown	
	To give the <body> element (the visible part of the Web page) a pale yellow background color.
Type **}**	To close the style rule.

7	Choose **File, Save**	To open the Save As dialog box.
	Double-click the **styles** folder	To open it. You'll save the style sheet in this folder.

ACA objective 5.8a

Tell students that this is just an example of a logical file name they might choose.

	In the File name box, type **globalstyles.css**	File name: globalstyles.css
	Click **Save**	(Or press Enter.) To save the style sheet.
8	Choose **Window, CSS Styles**	To open the CSS Styles panel.
	Click All	(If necessary.) To display the style sheet reference.
	To the left of the style sheet, click as shown	
		(If necessary.) To expand the style sheet. The rule you created for the `<body>` element appears.

If the Files panel is now too small, tell students to close the Insert panel and expand the Files panel by dragging up from its top border.

9	Open index.html	(From the Files panel.) You'll attach the style sheet to this page.
	Observe the CSS Styles panel	The style sheet does not appear because this page is not linked to it.
10	Click	(The Attach Style Sheet button is at the bottom of the CSS Styles panel.) The Attach External Style Sheet dialog box appears.
	Click **Browse**	To open the Select Style Sheet File dialog box.
	Open the styles folder	

ACA objective 5.2g

11	Select **globalstyles.css**	
	Click **OK**	To attach the style sheet to this page and close the Select Style Sheet File dialog box.
	Verify that **Link** is selected	To create a link to this style sheet.
	Click **OK**	To close the Attach External Style Sheet dialog box. The page now has a pale yellow background because the color is applied to the `<body>` element in the style sheet. You'll edit this style in the CSS Styles panel.

This background color doesn't work well with the white background of the images, so students will change this style.

	12 Switch to Code view	
Point out that Dreamweaver helps users focus on the pages and their relationships, rather than on the code.	Locate the link to the style sheet	(Around line 6.) The code now includes a link to globalstyles.css.
	Switch to Design view	
	13 Collapse the Insert panel	(Double-click to the right of the Insert tab.) To show more of the CSS Styles panel.
ACA objective 5.3b	14 In the CSS Styles panel, click **body**	To select the rule.
⚠ *Point out that if students applied a different color value earlier, the hexadecimal value will be different.*	Click **#FFC**	To edit this color value.
	Type **#fff** and press (↵ ENTER)	To change the background color to white. This is one way you can quickly edit style rules.
Case does not matter in color values.	15 Open products.html	From the Files panel.
	In the CSS Styles panel, click ▢	To open the Attach External Style Sheet dialog box, which is automatically populated with the correct path and file name.
	Click **OK**	To attach the page to the style sheet.
ACA objective 6.5g	16 Observe the Related Files toolbar	(Under the Document tab.) Globalstyles.css is displayed because it's now attached to the page. You can click the style sheet name to open the file.
	17 Save and close products.html	(If prompted, save globalstyles.css.) In the next activity, you'll continue to modify the index.html page and the style sheet.

Typography basics

Explanation
There are many typographical styles that you can apply to text, including the font (typeface), font size, and weight (degree of boldness).

Font-size units

To control font size, there are several units of measurement you can use, including points and pixels. Points are a unit of print measurement that does not translate well to the screen. Pixels are a more appropriate choice for the Web. Using pixels typically produces the most consistent results across various browsers and platforms.

Font sets

ACA objectives 5.3a, 2.1b, 2.1h
A *font set* is a list of similar fonts. When you apply a font set, the user's Web browser tries to display text in the first font specified in the set. If the first font isn't available on the user's computer, the browser looks for the second font in the set. If that font isn't available, the browser tries to apply the third font in the set, and so on. A font set should end with a generic font—serif, sans serif, or monospaced. This practice guarantees that even if a user doesn't have any of the fonts listed in your font set, at least the general font type will be applied.

Serif and sans serif fonts

The difference between serif and sans serif fonts is the style in which the letters are formed. A serif font has *flourishes* (decorations) at the ends of its characters, while sans serif fonts don't, as illustrated in Exhibit 3-6. In monospaced fonts, such as Courier and Courier New, each character takes up the same amount of horizontal space. Monospaced fonts resemble typewriter text.

Exhibit 3-6: Serif and sans serif fonts

Creating and applying element styles

ACA objectives 2.1b, 5.1b, 5.8c
You can define the appearance of an HTML element by using the HTML tag name as the selector in the style rule. When you define an element style in a global style sheet, every instance of that element across the site will pick up the style. This feature helps to ensure a consistent appearance and makes style updates fast and easy.

To use the CSS Styles panel to create an element style:

1 Open the Web page or style sheet.

ACA objective 5.8e
2 In the CSS Styles panel, click the New CSS Rule button.

3 From the Selector Type list, select Tag.

4 From the Selector Name list, select the HTML tag (element) to which you want to apply the style.

5 Under Rule Definition, do one of the following:

- Select the style sheet in which you want to write the new style. (This option will not be displayed if the active document is a style sheet.)
- Select (New Style Sheet File) if you want to write the style in a new style sheet.
- Select (This document only) if you want to embed the style in the active document. If you select this option with a Web page active, the style will be applied to that page only.

6 Click OK.

7 In the CSS Rule Definition dialog box, set the desired attributes for the style.

8 Click OK.

Creating and editing styles in the Property inspector

ACA objective 5.2h

The Property inspector provides another way to quickly apply new styles to your pages. Click the CSS button, shown in Exhibit 3-7, to display the CSS options. Then, either select a rule from the Targeted Rule list, or create a rule. Click the Edit Rule button to open the CSS Rule Definition dialog box for the selected rule. You can also quickly apply some of the most common styles, including font, font size, color, and text alignment.

Exhibit 3-7: CSS rule controls in the Property inspector

CSS style inheritance

ACA objective 2.1h

An HTML element can inherit the CSS styles of its parent element (the element that contains it). For example, if you apply font styles to the `<body>` element, every element on the page will inherit those styles because the `<body>` element is the parent element of every rendered element on the page. Similarly, if you have a `<div>` tag that contains three paragraphs (`<p>` tags), and you apply font and color styles to the `<div>` tag, those three paragraphs will inherit the styles.

As you apply styles to your pages, you can use inheritance to your advantage. Inheritance helps eliminate redundancy and complexity, resulting in smaller and more efficient style sheets that are easy to update. Inheritance is also referred to as the "cascade," hence the name Cascading Style Sheets (CSS).

There are some exceptions to the general rule of style inheritance. Not every CSS property can be inherited, and some elements, like headings, have their own default font sizes. To change the font size of a heading, you need to apply styles directly to the heading tag by creating an element style.

Do it! **B-3: Defining element styles**

Here's how	Here's why
The index.html page is open.	
1 In the Property inspector, click **CSS**	To display the CSS options.
ACA objective 5.2h	
In the Targeted Rule box, verify that **body** is selected	Targeted Rule **body**
	You'll apply styles to the `<body>` element, and these styles will be inherited by all other elements in the document.
ACA objectives 5.3a, 5.3b	
2 From the Font list, select **Verdana, Geneva, sans-serif**	The text on the page changes to the new font because every element inherits the styles of the `<body>` element, the topmost parent element.
Tell students that pixels are the default unit of measurement.	
From the Size list, select **12**	Size: **12** pixels
	To set the size of the body text to 12 pixels. The text on the page is smaller, except for the headings.
Facilitate a brief discussion.	
3 Why don't the headings inherit the font size of the body rule?	*Browsers apply their own default font size to text defined as a heading. To change the font size of a heading, you need to apply the style directly to it.*
4 In the CSS Styles panel, click	(The New CSS Rule button.) The New CSS Rule dialog box opens. You'll create a style rule for all level-one headings.
Under Selector Type, select **Tag**	You'll define an element style, meaning that it applies to all instances of a specific HTML tag.
From the Selector Name list, select **h1**	(If necessary.) To apply this rule to the `<h1>` element.
Under Rule Definition, verify that **globalstyles.css** is selected	This rule will apply to all level-one headings on pages attached to this style sheet.
Click **OK**	The CSS Rule Definition dialog box opens.
5 In the Font-size box, type **20**	To give all level-one headings a font size of 20 pixels.
6 Click the Color box	To open the color palette.
Select a dark green color	
Click **OK**	To apply the new style. The two level-one headings on the page are now green and smaller than their default size.

7	Scroll down the page to view the Awards heading	This heading did not pick up the style because it's a level-two heading, defined by the `<h2>` element.
8	Open the New CSS Rule dialog box	In the CSS Styles panel, click the Create New CSS Rule button.
	From the Selector Type list, select **Tag**	
	From the Selector Name list, select **h2** and click **OK**	To create a style rule for level-two headings.
9	From the Font-size list, select **16**	
	Apply a brown text color	Click the Color box and select a brown color from the palette.
	Click **OK**	To apply the new element style.
10	Observe the CSS Styles panel	The h1 and h2 rules appear in the style tree, and the properties of the selected rule are displayed.
11	On the Related Files toolbar, click **globalstyles.css**	

To view the changes in the style sheet.

	Observe the new CSS code	You can modify the CSS code directly in the style sheet, or you can use the Property inspector and the CSS Styles panel to create and edit styles.
	Choose **File**, **Save**	To save your changes in the style sheet.
12	Click **Source Code**	(On the Related Files toolbar.) To display the code for the index.html page.
	Switch to Design view	

TIPS *Tell students they can also press Ctrl+S.*

Class styles

Explanation

Class styles allow you to share styles among different HTML elements and to name your elements, thus giving added meaning to your document structure. For example, let's say you want to apply a style to just one paragraph among several. You can't achieve this by changing the style definition for the <p> tag, because that will affect *all* paragraphs. Instead, you can create a class style and apply it to only the paragraph where it's needed.

Class names

ACA objectives 2.1d, 5.8e, 2.1h

Give your class styles meaningful names to make maintenance easier, both for you and for others who might work on the site in the future. For example, a year from now, it'll be easier to determine how a class style was meant to be used if it's named "discount" instead of "class2."

Creating class styles

As with all CSS styles, you can create class styles in internal or external style sheets. To create a class style:

1 Open the Web page or style sheet.
2 In the CSS Styles panel, click the New CSS Rule button.
3 In the New CSS Rule dialog box, under Selector Type, select Class.
4 In the Name box, type a meaningful name. (Class styles must begin with a period, and Dreamweaver automatically adds the period before the class name.)
5 Under Rule Definition, do one of the following:
    • Select the style sheet in which you want to write the new style. (This option will not be displayed if the active document is a style sheet.)
    • Select (New Style Sheet File) if you want to write the style in a new style sheet.
    • Select (This document only) if you want to write the style in the active document. If you select this option with a Web page active, the style will be embedded in the page's <head> section and will be applied to that page only.
6 Click OK.
7 In the CSS Rule Definition dialog box, define the attributes for the style.
8 Click OK.

Applying class styles

After you create a class style, you need to apply it to one or more elements. The class styles you create appear in the Targeted Rule list in the Property inspector. To apply a class style, select an element on the page and then select the class style from the Targeted Rule list.

Do it!

B-4: Creating and applying class styles

Here's how	Here's why
1 Create a new CSS rule	In the CSS Styles panel, click the New CSS Rule button.
ACA objective 5.8e From the Selector Type list, select **Class**	
Tell students that they can enter the period themselves or let Dreamweaver add it. In the Selector Name box, type **copyright**	To specify a meaningful name that reflects how the style will be used. Class names begin with a period, but you don't have to type it here because Dreamweaver adds it automatically in the code.
2 In the Rule Definition list, verify that **globalstyles.css** is selected	
Click **OK**	To open the CSS Rule Definition dialog box.
ACA objective 5.3b 3 In the Font-size box, type **11**	The copyright class style will apply a font size of 11 pixels.
From the Font-style list, select **italic**	The copyright class style will also make text italic.
4 Click the Color box	To open the color palette.
Select the white color swatch	(The hexadecimal code that appears should be #FFF.) To make the text white. This means you'll need to change the background color so that there's sufficient contrast to read the white text.
5 Under Category, select **Background**	To display the background style options.
Click the Background-color box	To open the color palette.
Select the dark green color **#060**	This dark green color will provide sufficient contrast to read the white text in the copyright statement.
6 Click **OK**	To create the copyright class style.
7 In the Document window, scroll to the bottom of the page	
Click in the copyright text	

	8 In the Property inspector, from the Targeted Rule list, select **copyright**	To apply the new class style to the text. The copyright statement now has a green background, with smaller, white, italic text.
	Switch to Split view	
Point out that the class style is applied to the table cell that contains the copyright text.	Observe the code for the copyright text	`<td class="copyright">&copy;`
		The class style is applied by using the `class` attribute. In this case, the copyright text is contained in a table cell (the `<td>` tag.)
	Switch to Design view	
	9 Observe the CSS Styles panel	The properties in the copyright style rule are displayed.
	10 In the Property inspector, click ▤	To center the text.
	Observe the CSS Styles panel	The text-align property appears at the bottom of the properties list for the copyright style.
	11 Create a class style named **navbar**	Click the New CSS Rule button, verify that Class is selected, type "navbar" in the Selector Name box, and click OK.
	12 Under Category, select **Background**	
	Click the Background-color box	
	Select a light green color, such as #6C3	The green color #6C3 is on the right side of the color palette.
	Click **OK**	To create the navbar style.
	13 Click anywhere in the navigation links at the top of the page	
	In the tag selector, click **\<td\>**, as shown	`<body> <table> <tr> <td> <a>` PROPERTIES ◇ HTML Targeted Rule
		To select the table cell that contains the navigation links. You'll apply the navbar style to this element.
Links are covered elsewhere in the course.	14 From the Targeted Rule list, select **navbar**	(In the Property inspector.) To apply the new class style to the table cell that contains the links.
	15 Save your changes in index.html and globalstyles.css	

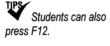
16 Click the Preview/Debug in
    Browser button

    Choose **Preview in IExplore**

    Close the browser, and close all
    open files in Dreamweaver

Unit summary: Structure and style

Topic A   In this topic, you learned how to apply **structural tags**, including headings and paragraphs. You also learned that an efficient and meaningful page structure can make it easier to maintain a Web site, as well as to design and arrange page content. Then, you learned how to create unordered, ordered, and nested **lists**.

Topic B   In this topic, you learned about **Cascading Style Sheets (CSS)**. You learned about the differences between internal and external style sheets, and you learned basic CSS syntax. Then you learned how to create an external style sheet and link documents to it. Finally, you learned how to define **element styles** and how to create and apply **class styles**.

Independent practice activity

In this activity, you'll attach a style sheet to several pages, define element styles, and create and apply a class style.

The files for this activity are in Student Data folder **Unit 3\Unit summary**.

1 Define a new site named **Text Practice**, using the Outlander Spices folder as the site's root directory.

2 Open index.html.

3 Attach globalstyles.css to index.html. (*Hint:* The style sheet is in the styles subfolder.)

4 Define the text "Awards" as a level-two heading.

5 In globalstyles.css, create a class style named **mission** that makes text **bold** and **italic**, with a font size of **14 pixels**.

6 Apply the new style to the top paragraph in index.html.

7 Open recipes.html and attach globalstyles.css to it.

8 Define a new CSS style for the `<ul>` (unordered list) element. (*Hint:* In the New CSS Rule dialog box, select **Tag**, and then select **ul** from the Selector Name list.)

9 Set the font size to **12 pixels**, and the text color to a dark green. Verify the changes in recipes.html.

10 Define a new CSS style for the `<ol>` (ordered list) element.

11 Set the font size to **12 pixels**, and the text color to a dark brown. Verify the changes in recipes.html.

12 Save the page and preview it in your browser. When you're done, close the browser to return to Dreamweaver.

13 Save and close all open files.

Review questions

1 If you want all of the level-two headings in your site to share the same formatting, you should:

    A Create an internal element style for the <h2> tag.

    B Create an external element style for the <h2> tag.

    C Create an internal class style.

    D Create an external class style.

2 If you want to create a special type of paragraph with extra large text, and you think you'll need to use the style for multiple paragraphs on a page, it's best to:

    A Create an internal element style for the <p> tag.

    B Create an external element style for the <p> tag.

    c Create an external class style and give it a meaningful name.

    D Create an external ID style and give it a meaningful name.

3 If you want to define a unique section that holds the navigation bar and you want this element to look the same on every page, it's best to:

    A Create an internal class style and give it a meaningful name, such as navbar.

    B Create an external class style and give it a meaningful name, such as navbar.

    C Create an internal ID style and give it a meaningful name, such as navbar.

    D Create an external ID style and give it a meaningful name, such as navbar.

4 How can you change the font size in a CSS style? [Choose all that apply.]

    A In the CSS Styles panel, select the style. Click the Edit Rule button, make the change, and click OK.

    B In the CSS Styles panel, select the style. Click the value next to font-size in the list of properties, and then edit the value.

    C Double-click some text with the style applied. In the dialog box, change the font size and click OK.

    D Edit the font size directly in the style sheet file.

5 True or false? A class named "introduction" is likely to be more meaningful and effective than a class named "style3."

    True. It's important that you give your class styles meaningful names that reflect their role in the document structure.

6 True or false? When you create a style for the <h1> element for a page that contains that element, all you need to do is define the style and it's applied automatically.

    True. When you define element styles, they are applied automatically.

7 True or false? When you create a class style, the style is automatically applied on the page.

    False. After you define a class style, you have to apply it to one or more page elements.

Unit 4
Tables

Unit time: 45 minutes

Complete this unit, and you'll know how to:

A Create and modify tables, write effective table summaries, and create nested tables.

B Format rows and cells, merge cells, add rows and columns, apply fixed and variable widths, and change cell borders and padding.

Topic A: Creating tables

This topic covers the following Adobe ACA exam objectives for Dreamweaver CS5.

#	Objective
2.4c	Identify specific techniques used to make a website accessible to viewers with visual and motor impairments.
4.9a	Demonstrate knowledge of how to import tabular data.
4.9b	Demonstrate knowledge of table, cell, row, and column properties.
4.9c	Demonstrate knowledge of how to set and change table, cell, row, and column properties.

Basic tables

Explanation

An HTML table is a grid structure of rows and columns that you can use to display tabular data, such as products and prices, or to arrange page elements. Tables can be nested inside other tables to create more complex grid structures.

Tables are generally meant for data that's best arranged in rows and columns, such as the information shown in Exhibit 4-1. You can also use tables to arrange page content into a layout, but it's generally best to use CSS to achieve layout and style objectives.

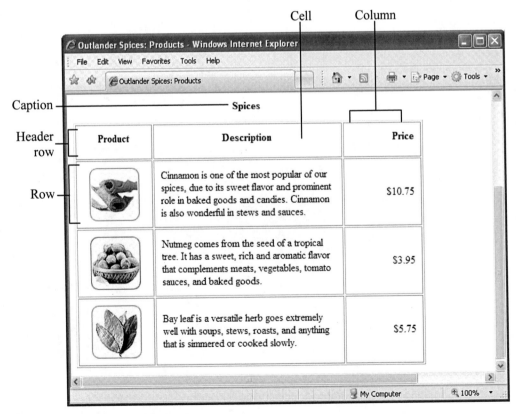

Exhibit 4-1: A simple table used to arrange content

Inserting a table

To insert a table, drag the Table icon from the Insert panel to the page. When the Table dialog box, shown in Exhibit 4-2, opens, define the basic table settings. You can then use the Property inspector to change table properties as needed. After you've created a table, you can drag text and images into the cells.

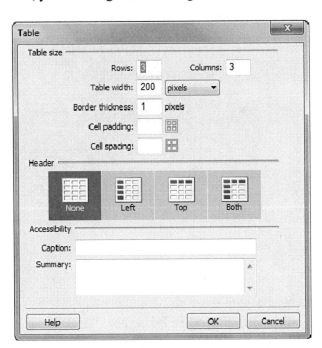

Exhibit 4-2: The Table dialog box

The following table describes the options in the Table dialog box.

	Option	Description
ACA objective 4.9b	Rows	Defines the number of rows in the table.
	Columns	Defines the number of columns in the table.
	Table width	Defines the width of the table, either in pixels or as a percentage of the browser window or a containing element, such as a `<div>` element.
	Border thickness	Defines the width of the cell borders.
	Cell padding	Defines the amount of space between a cell's contents and the cell's border.
	Cell spacing	Defines the amount of space between adjacent cells.
	Header	Defines whether the left column or top row, or both, will be used as row or column headers.
	Caption	Defines a title that describes the table.
ACA objective 2.4c	Summary	Provides a description of the table's contents that can be read by screen readers for the visually impaired.

Importing tabular data

ACA objective 4.9a
You can also create tables by importing data from other sources, such as text files that separate data with tabs, commas, or other delimiters. Here's how:

1 Choose File, Import, Tabular Data to open the Import Tabular Data dialog box, shown in Exhibit 4-3.

2 Click Browse and navigate to the file that contains the data you want to import.

3 From the Delimiter list, select the delimiter that separates each unit of data in the file.

4 Set formatting options if necessary, and click OK.

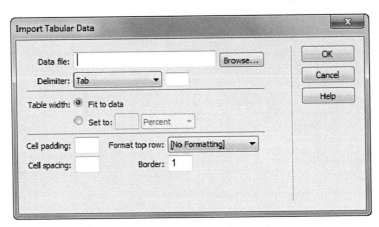

Exhibit 4-3: The Import Tabular Data dialog box

Visual aids

When you're working with tables, you might find it helpful to enable (or disable) the two table-related visual aids, Table Widths and Table Borders. If you activate the Table Widths visual aid, the current table width is displayed at the bottom of the table, as shown in Exhibit 4-4. You can click the value or the triangles to display a menu.

The Table Widths visual aid is active by default. If you want to disable it, click the Visual Aids button on the Document toolbar. A checkmark appears next to each active visual aid. Select Table Widths to disable that visual aid. (If there is no checkmark next to the visual aid, selecting it activates it.)

The Table Borders visual aid draws dotted lines around the table grid so that you can more easily work with the table rows and columns. This visual aid appears only in Design view and will not appear when the page is viewed in a browser.

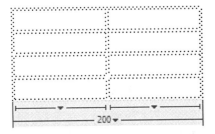

Exhibit 4-4: The Table Borders and Table Widths visual aids

Table summaries

ACA objective 2.4c

When you create a table, you should always specify a table summary. A summary is not displayed in a visual browser; it benefits users who access Web content using alternative devices such as screen readers. Summaries provide important information and context for these users. For example, an effective table summary might read, "This table contains a list of spices in separate rows, with descriptions and prices for each spice." This summary provides an overview of the table content before the screen reader reads aloud the table content.

Do it!

A-1: Creating a table

Here's how	Here's why
1 Choose **Site, New Site...**	To open the Site Setup dialog box.
2 In the Site Name box, type **Outlander Tables**	To name the site.
3 Browse to the current topic folder	
Open the Outlander Spices folder, click **Select**, and click **Save**	To set the root folder for this site and create the site.
4 Expand the Insert panel	(If necessary.) Double-click to the right of the Insert tab.
Collapse the CSS Styles panel	(If necessary.) You won't use this panel in this topic.
5 From the Files panel, open products.html	The page is blank. You'll create a basic table and add text and images to it.
From the Insert panel, drag 🔲 onto the blank page	The Table dialog box appears.
Edit the Rows box to read **4**	To set the number of table rows to four.
Edit the Columns box to read **2**	To set the number of columns to two.
6 Edit the Table width box to read **580**	To set the table width to 580 pixels.
7 Edit the Border thickness box to read **0**	(Zero.) You'll rely on the Table Borders visual aid to see the table gridlines.
8 Under Header, click **Top**	
	To make the top row of the table a header row.

Have students verify that Pixels is selected.

ACA objectives 4.9b, 4.9c

ACA objective 2.4c

9 In the Summary box, type **This table lists various spices and their descriptions.**

To create a brief summary that describes the content of this table for screen readers and other alternative devices.

Click **OK**

To create the table. The table width is shown at the bottom of the table. You'll hide the table width information.

10 On the Document toolbar, click

To display the Visual Aids list.

Select **Table Widths**

To hide the table width information.

11 Click

To display the Visual Aids list again.

Select **Table Borders**

To hide the dotted lines that identify the table gridlines. Without this visual aid, it's difficult to work with the table, so you'll activate it again.

12 Re-activate the Table Borders visual aid

So that you can see the table gridlines while you work. This border will not appear in a browser.

13 Click in the top-left table cell

To place the insertion point.

Tell students that they can change these default styles with CSS.

Type **Product**

To create a heading for this column. The text in this row is bold and centered in each cell because that's the default formatting of the `<th>` (table header) element, which defines each cell in this row. (You specified the top row of the table as a header in the Table dialog box.)

14 Click in the top-right cell

Type **Description**

To create a heading for the right column.

15 In the Files panel, expand the images folder

You'll add spice images to the table.

Drag **cinnamon.jpg** into the cell under "Product," as shown

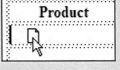

The Image Tag Accessibility Attributes dialog box opens.

ACA objective 2.4c

In the Alternate text box, enter **Cinnamon**

To specify alternate text for this image. This text allows users with non-visual devices, such as screen readers, to understand the content or purpose of the image.

Click **OK**

To insert the image.

16 Insert **bayleaf.jpg** and **cloves.jpg** into the Product cells, as shown

Enter appropriate alternate text for each image.

Collapse the images folder

(In the Files panel.) To view the files in the Site folder.

17 Open descriptions.txt

(In the Files panel, double-click descriptions.txt.) You'll insert text from this file into the Description column.

TIPS✓ *Tell students to use Ctrl+C to copy the text and Ctrl+V to paste it.*

Select and copy the cinnamon description

18 Switch to products.html

Paste the text into the cell next to the cinnamon image

19 Copy the other descriptions into their corresponding cells

Select each description, copy it, and paste it into the appropriate cell. The column width changes as you add the text.

Tell students that they will continue to build the table in the next activity.

Close descriptions.txt

20 Save products.html

Nested tables

Explanation

A *nested table* is a table that's inserted into the cell of another table. Nested tables give you more flexibility in arranging content, so they're often used to achieve a particular page layout or section layout.

In Exhibit 4-5, for example, the outer table contains all the content shown, and the nested table contains text in cells to be used to create a navigation bar. The outer table consists of one column and two rows. The nested table is placed in the second row of the outer table and consists of one row and six columns.

Exhibit 4-5: A nested table used for layout purposes

Layout table summaries

ACA objective 2.4c

When a table is used for layout purposes and not to structure data, you should briefly indicate this in the table's summary so that users with screen readers and other alternative devices will understand the purpose or context of the table before they begin to read its content.

Do it!

A-2:   Creating a nested table

Here's how	Here's why
1 Drag ⊞ to the space above the table, as shown	(From the Insert panel.) To insert another table. The Table dialog box appears.
2 Set the number of Rows to **2** and the number of Columns to **1**	
Set the table width to **705**	
Set the border thickness to **0**	(If necessary.) You'll continue to rely on the Table Borders visual aid to see the table gridlines.
Under Header, click **None**, and click **OK**	You don't need a header row for this table.

3 In the top row of the new table, insert logo.gif

In the Files panel, expand the images folder, and drag logo.gif into the top row of the table.

ACA objective 2.4c

In the Alternate text box, type **Outlander Spices logo**

Click **OK**

Collapse the images folder

4 Drag 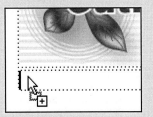 to the bottom row of the table, as shown

To insert another table inside the cell of the existing table. The Table dialog box appears.

Set the number of Rows to **1** and the number of Columns to **6**

Verify that the Table width is set to **705**

Verify that the border thickness is set to **0**

ACA objective 2.4c

5 In the Summary box, type **Layout table for site links**

To create a summary that describes the purpose of this table for screen readers and other alternative devices.

Click **OK**

6 Click the first cell of the nested table and type **Home**

This will serve as the Home link for the navigation bar.

Press (TAB)

To go to the next cell.

7 In the remaining cells, enter:
About Us
Locations
Products
Recipes
Contact

Press Tab after each item.

8 Save and close all open files

Topic B: Table structure and formatting

This topic covers the following Adobe ACA exam objectives for Dreamweaver CS5.

#	Objective
2.1f	Demonstrate knowledge of fixed and flexible page sizing.
4.9b	Demonstrate knowledge of table, cell, row, and column properties.
4.9c	Demonstrate knowledge of how to set and change table, cell, row, and column properties.
4.9d	Demonstrate knowledge of sizing methods used for tables.
4.9e	Demonstrate knowledge of how to insert and delete columns and rows.
4.9f	Demonstrate knowledge of how to merge and split cells.
5.6a	Demonstrate knowledge of HTML tags.

Basic table structure

Explanation

Now that you know how to create tables and add text and images to them, you'll learn how to modify a table's structure and apply basic formatting. To do so, you'll need to know how to select table components, and it will be helpful if you're familiar with the table-related HTML tags.

ACA objective 5.6a

The `<table>` tag defines a table. Within the `<table>` tag, each `<tr>` tag defines a row, and within each row, `<td>` tags define each cell. The number of cells in a row determines the number of columns in the table. For example, Exhibit 4-6 shows the code for a table consisting of two rows—notice the two sets of `<tr>` tags—and three columns. The resulting table is shown on the right.

```
<table>
    <tr>
        <td> </td>
        <td> </td>
        <td> </td>
    </tr>

    <tr>
        <td> </td>
        <td> </td>
        <td> </td>
    </tr>
</table>
```

Exhibit 4-6: A simple two-row, three-column table

You can select all the cells in a column or row, or select individual cells. You must select a row, column, or cell before you can set properties for it.

Selecting individual table cells

The easiest and fastest way to select an individual cell is to press Ctrl and click the cell. You can also click in a cell and then click the rightmost <td> tag in the tag selector at the bottom of the Document window.

Selecting rows or columns

To select a row or column, do any of the following:

- Point to the left edge of the leftmost cell (for a row) or the top edge of the topmost cell (for a column). When the pointer changes to a position arrow, click to select the row or column.
- Click the left cell of a row and drag to the right, or click the top cell of a column and drag down.
- (Rows only) Click the cell and then click the rightmost <tr> tag in the tag selector.
- (Rows only) Switch to Code view and select all of the content between a <tr> tag and its corresponding </tr> tag.

Formatting rows

ACA objective 4.9c

Once you have selected a row, you can use the Property inspector to apply formatting. The row formatting options, shown in Exhibit 4-7, are displayed in the bottom section of the Property inspector. If the bottom section of the Property inspector is not displayed, click the triangle in the lower-right corner of the panel to expand it.

Exhibit 4-7: The row formatting options in the Property inspector

ACA objective 4.9f

Using row formatting options, you can:

- Merge adjacent cells into a single cell.
- Split a cell into multiple rows or columns.
- Change the horizontal and vertical alignment of content in the cells in the selected row.
- Change the width and height of the selected row.
- Prevent the text in the cells from wrapping to a new line.
- Define the selected row as a table header row.
- Apply a background color.

Do it!

B-1: Selecting and formatting rows

The files for this activity are in Student Data folder **Unit 4\Topic B**.

Here's how	Here's why
1 Choose **Site, New Site...**	To open the Site Setup dialog box.
2 In the Site Name box, type **Outlander Tables 2**	
3 Browse to the current topic folder	
Open the Outlander Spices folder, click **Select**, and click **Save**	To set the root folder for this site and create the site.
4 Open products.html	From the Files panel.

TIPS
Students can also select the row by clicking the first cell and dragging to the right, or by clicking the <tr> tag in the tag selector.

5 In the product table, point to the left edge of the top-left cell and click once, as shown

Product	
	Cinnamon is one of t prominent role in bak and sauces.

(Make sure that the pointer changes to a right-pointing arrow before you click.) To select the row. You'll format this row.

ACA objectives 4.9b, 4.9c

In the Property inspector, from the Vert list, select **Top** — To align the text vertically to the top of the row.

Help students with this step, if necessary.

6 Drag to select the remaining two product rows — (Point to the left edge of the second row. When the pointer changes to an arrow, drag down to select the other two product rows.) You'll apply the same formatting to these rows.

7 Set the vertical alignment to the top

8 Save your changes

Modifying cells

Explanation

ACA objectives 4.9c, 4.9f

There are several ways you can modify table cells by using the Property inspector. When multiple rows or cells are selected, you can merge them. When a single cell is selected, you can split it to create new rows or columns. You can also control cell width, apply background colors to individual cells, rows, or columns, and insert new rows and columns.

Changing cell width

When you change the width of a cell, the entire column is affected. By default, columns are sized according to the largest cell in each column, which is determined by the size of the content it contains. You can also set specific column widths in pixels or as percentage values.

Specifying background colors

You can specify a background color for rows, columns, and individual cells. To do so, select the row, column, or cell, and then click the Bg box in the Property inspector to open a color palette. Click a swatch to apply its color.

Inserting and deleting rows and columns

ACA objective 4.9e

When a single cell is selected, you can add a row of cells above or below it, and you can add a column to the right or left of it.

To insert a new row in a table, do any of the following:

- Select a cell and choose Insert, Table Objects, Insert Row Above or Insert Row Below.
- Right-click a cell and choose Table, Insert Row. (The row is inserted above the selected cell.)
- Right-click a cell and choose Table, Insert Rows or Columns. In the dialog box, apply the desired settings and click OK.

To insert a column, do any of the following:

- Select a cell and choose Insert, Table Objects, Insert Column to the Left or Insert Column to the Right.
- Right-click a cell and choose Table, Insert Column. (The column is inserted to the left of the selected cell.)
- Right-click a cell and choose Table, Insert Rows or Columns. In the dialog box, apply the desired settings and click OK.

To delete a row:

- Click or select the row and choose Modify, Table, Delete Row.
- Right-click a row and choose Table, Delete Row.

To delete a column:

- Click or select the column and choose Modify, Table, Delete Column.
- Right-click a column and choose Table, Delete Column.

B-2: Inserting and formatting columns and rows

Here's how	Here's why
1 Click the cell containing the text "Description"	To place the insertion point.
2 Choose **Insert**, **Table Objects**, **Insert Column to the Right**	To add a column to the right of the cell.
3 Set the cell width to **100**	(In the Property inspector, enter 100 in the W box.) Changing the width of the cell affects the entire column. Column widths are set according to the largest cell in the column.
4 In the top cell in the new column, type **Price**	To create a column heading. The text is automatically formatted as a heading, like the other cells in this row.
In the remaining cells, from top to bottom, enter **$10.75**, **$3.95**, and **$5.75**	To enter price data for each spice.
5 Right-click a cell in the heading row and choose **Table**, **Insert Row**	To insert a row at the top of the table.
Select the new top row	Point to the left edge of the top-left cell in the Spices table until the pointer changes to an arrow, and then click.
In the Property inspector, click ⬚	To merge the row's cells into a single cell.
6 Click in the merged cell	To place the insertion point in the cell.
Type **Specials**	
In the H box, enter **30**	(In the Property inspector.) To specify a cell height of 30 pixels.
7 In the Property inspector, click the Bg box	To open a background-color palette.
Select the green color **#339900**	To give the cell a green background.
8 Save your changes	

ACA objectives 4.9b, 4.9c

TIPS *Students can also press Ctrl+M.*

ACA objective 4.9f

Students will continue to modify the table in the next activity.

Column widths and cell properties

Explanation

You can control column and table widths in a variety of ways. You can set column widths to a fixed size, or use percentage values to create variable widths. You can also customize cell borders, the space between adjacent cells, and the space between a cell's content and its borders.

Fixed and variable widths

ACA objectives 2.1f and 4.9d

You can set a column's width to a fixed number of pixels or to a percentage of the table width. Similarly, you can set a table's width to either fixed or variable. A variable-width table is sized with a percentage value and is relative to the width of the browser window. You can also combine fixed- and variable-width settings, as described in the following table.

If the column width is fixed, it stays the same size whether the table width is fixed or variable.

Column width	Table width	Resulting column width
100 pixels	500 pixels	100 pixels
100 pixels	85% (of browser)	100 pixels
10% (of table)	500 pixels	50 pixels (10% of 500 pixels)
10% (of table)	85% (of browser)	8.5% of browser (10% of 85%)

Do it!

B-3: Applying fixed and variable widths

Here's how	Here's why
1 Preview products.html in your browser	You'll change some of the columns from fixed widths to variable widths.
Point to the right edge of the browser window	The pointer changes to a double-sided arrow to enable resizing.
Drag the right edge of the window back and forth	To resize the window. Notice that the tables remain the same size. They have fixed widths, so their size isn't calculated relative to the size of the browser window.
Close the browser	
2 Click in the Product cell	
ACA objective 4.9d In the W box, enter **100**	(In the Property inspector.) To set the width of the first column to 100 pixels.
ACA objective 5.6a 3 In the tag selector, click **\<table\>**	`<body> <table> <tr> <th>` `PROPERTIES` To select the entire table. You'll change the width of the table from a fixed width to a percentage of the browser window. The options in the Property inspector change with the selection.
ACA objective 2.1f In the W box, enter **85**	`W  85  %`
From the adjacent list, select **%**	To make the table width 85% of the width of the browser window.

TIPS Tell students they can also hold down the Ctrl key and click each cell.

4 Drag to select from the **Price** header to the last price data cell	

You'll align the price data in this column.

ACA objectives 4.9b, 4.9c   5 From the Horz list, select **Center** (In the Property inspector.) To center the data horizontally in these cells.

Point out that flexible tables are a design option that is effective in some circumstances and not in others.

6	Center the spice images in their cells	Drag to select the cells, and then select Center from the Horz list in the Property inspector.
7	Click in the Description cell	
	From the Horz list, select **Left**	To align this table header to the left of its cell.
8	Save the page and preview it in your browser	
	Resize the browser window horizontally	Drag the edge of the window back and forth. The product table expands and contracts as the window changes size. However, the right and left columns in the table remain the same size because they have fixed widths.
	Close the browser	
9	Click inside the product table	
	In the tag selector, click **<table>**	To select the product table.
10	Set the table width to **710** pixels	In the Property inspector, enter 710 in the W box, and then select pixels from the adjacent list.

Borders, cell spacing, and cell padding

Explanation

Dreamweaver applies default settings to table borders, the spacing inside cells, and the spacing between cell borders and cell content. You can modify these attributes by selecting the table and then setting options in the Property inspector.

ACA objectives 4.9b, 4.9c

The space between a cell's borders and its content is called *cell padding*. You can change the amount of cell padding by selecting the table and entering a numeric value in the CellPad box in the Property inspector. The space between adjacent cells is called *cell spacing*. You can change the amount of cell spacing by selecting the table and entering a value in the CellSpace box in the Property inspector.

Do it!

B-4:   Customizing table cell properties

Here's how	Here's why
1 Select the product table	(If necessary.) You'll adjust the cell padding and borders.
2 In the Property inspector, in the CellPad box, enter **10**	To increase the space between each cell's border and its content to 10 pixels.
In the CellSpace box, enter **4**	To increase the space between adjacent cells to 4 pixels. You can see the increased space between the gridlines.
3 Edit the Border box to read **1**	To apply a 1-pixel border.
Edit the CellSpace box to read **0**	To remove the space between adjacent cells.
4 Save the page and preview it in Internet Explorer	
Close the browser	
Close products.html	

ACA objectives 4.9b, 4.9c

Unit summary: Tables

Topic A   In this topic, you learned about tables. You learned how to **insert a table**, create a header row, insert text and images, **import** tabular data, write effective table summaries, and create nested tables.

Topic B   In this topic, you learned how to select and format **cells**, **rows**, and **columns**. You learned how to merge cells and insert rows and columns. Finally, you learned how to fine-tune **table properties**, including column and table widths, borders, cell padding, and cell spacing.

Independent practice activity

In this activity, you'll create a table from an example.

The files for this activity are in Student Data folder **Unit 4\Unit summary**.

1 Open locations.html.

2 Below the USA image, create the table shown in Exhibit 4-8. Apply a background color of your choice to the heading row.

3 Save and close the page.

The shaded states indicate expansion plans over the next five years.

STATE	STORES AND LOCATIONS
Washington	• Seattle Blue Heaven • Sierra Foods, Medford • Shopper's Paradise, Seattle • Tacoma Treasure, Redmond
Oregon	• Port Plaza, Portland • Shopper's Paradise, Portland
Nevada	• All U Need, Reno • Plaza Givo, Las Vegas

Exhibit 4-8: The completed table

Review questions

1 What determines the number of columns in a table?

   A The number of rows

   B The number of column tags

   C The number of cells in each row

   D The value of the column attributes

2 What determines the width of a column?

   A The width you set for the first cell in the column

   B The width you set for the table

   C The width you set for an intersecting row

   D The width of the largest cell in that column

3 A table has a fixed width of 600 pixels. A cell inside this table has a width of 20%, and no other width is specified for another cell in its column. How many pixels wide is this column?

   A 80 pixels

   B 60 pixels

   C 160 pixels

   D 180 pixels

   E 120 pixels

4 What is cell padding?

   A The space between a cell's borders and content

   B The space between cells

   C The space between rows and columns

   D The space between a table and the bottom of the page

5 What is cell spacing?

   A The space between a cell's borders and content

   B The space between adjacent cells

   C The space between rows and columns

   D The space between a table and the bottom of the page

6 How can you delete a table row?

   A Click anywhere in the row and press the Delete key.

   B Click the row and choose Modify, Table, Delete Row.

   C Right-click the row and choose Delete.

   D Ctrl+click the row and press the Delete key.

Unit 5

Links

Unit time: 40 minutes

Complete this unit, and you'll know how to:

A Create links to other pages and resources, create named anchors and link to them, create e-mail links, and create an image map.

B Apply CSS styles to link states.

Topic A: Creating links

This topic covers the following Adobe ACA exam objectives for Dreamweaver CS5.

#	Objective
2.4a	List elements used to improve website usability.
2.4c	Identify specific techniques used to make a website accessible to viewers with visual and motor impairments.
4.5a	Demonstrate knowledge of the terms "hyperlink," "e-mail link," and "named anchor."
4.5b	Demonstrate knowledge of hyperlinks, including the differences between absolute, root-relative, and document-relative hyperlinks.
4.5c	Demonstrate knowledge of how to link text and images to another Web page of the same site.
4.5d	Demonstrate knowledge of how to link text and images to another website.
4.5e	Demonstrate knowledge of how to link text or images to an e-mail address.
4.5f	Demonstrate knowledge of how to create and link to a named anchor.
4.5g	Demonstrate knowledge of how to target links.
4.8a	Demonstrate knowledge of the terms "hotspot" and "image map" as used in Web page design.
4.8b	Demonstrate knowledge of how to create an image map.
4.8c	Identify best practices when creating image maps.
4.8d	Demonstrate knowledge of how to set properties for a hotspot by using the Property inspector.
4.10c	Demonstrate knowledge of how to link to a Word or Excel document from a Web page.
5.6a	Demonstrate knowledge of HTML tags.
6.5c	Demonstrate knowledge of how to link files by dragging, using the Point-to-File icon in the Property inspector and the Files panel.

Hyperlinks

Explanation

ACA objective 4.5a

Hyperlinks (usually called *links*) provide the functionality that makes the Web the interconnected world that it is. Links enable users to navigate to other pages in a site, to external pages and resources, and to specific sections of a page.

Link types

There are three basic link types:

- *Local* links navigate to other pages and resources in a Web site.
- *External* links navigate to pages and resources outside a Web site.
- *Named-anchor* links navigate to specific sections of a Web page. Named-anchor links are also called *bookmark links* or *intra-document links*.

Local links

Because local links are links to pages and resources within a Web site, specifying the path is usually simple. If the destination file resides in the same directory (folder) as the page that contains the link, you can simply type the file name in the Link box in the Property inspector.

ACA objective 4.5c

To create a local link:

1   Select the text or image that you want to serve as the link.

2   In the Property inspector, do one of the following:

- In the Link box, enter the name of the destination file. If the destination file is not in the same folder as the current page, enter the path and file name.

ACA objective 6.5c

- Next to the Link box, drag the Point-to-File icon to the destination file in the Files panel.

- Next to the Link box, click the Browse for File button (the folder icon), locate and select the destination file, and click OK.

ACA objective 4.10c

The preceding steps and options apply to any resource you link to, whether it's a Web page or another resource type such as a PDF, Word or Excel file.

The anchor tag

ACA objective 5.6a

Like any other elements, you can also create links manually in Code view. Links are defined by the `<a>` tag, which stands for anchor. The `href` attribute of this tag, which stands for "hypertext reference," determines the destination of the link. Using a simple example, the code for a link to your home page might read as follows:

```
<a href="index.html">Home</a>
```

Relative link addressing

ACA objective 4.5b

As mentioned earlier, if you're creating a link to a page or resource that's in the same folder as the page containing the link, you can simply type the file name in the Link box in the Property inspector. However, if the link destination resides in a different folder, you need to specify the folder name followed by a forward slash and then the file name; for example, `images/image1.gif`. This type of link is called a *document-relative* link.

The forward slash always takes you down one level in the folder hierarchy. If you need to link to a page or resource in a folder that's up a level in the folder hierarchy, you use two dots and a forward slash; for example, `../images/image1.gif`.

Depending on the standards you establish for your site's development, you might want to use *root-relative* link addresses. With this method of link addressing, you always specify the path all the way back to the site's root folder. This method can be useful if you frequently move files. For example, if you have a page with a root-relative link and then move the page to a different folder, the link remains valid as long as the destination page or resource has not moved.

Root-relative paths must start with a forward slash, which represents the site's root folder. For example, `/outlander/members/order.html` is a root–relative path to the file order.html, which is in the members folder in the site's root folder.

Link labels and link titles

ACA objectives 2.4a, 2.4c

Link text is sometimes called a *link label*; it should provide the user with a reasonable idea of what to expect when the link is clicked. For example, if you create a link for the text "download the menu in PDF format," that text provides sufficient information about the link, thereby enhancing the usability of the content. However, generic or out-of-context link labels such as "click here" or "this link," do not give the user an idea of what to expect if the link is clicked.

When your link text doesn't describe a link well enough, you can use a link title to provide more information about a link's destination page or resource. With the link text selected, enter a descriptive title in the Title box in the Property inspector. Screen readers also use link titles to provide context, which is an important aspect of Web site accessibility.

Do it!

A-1: Creating a link to a page in your site

The files for this activity are in Student Data folder **Unit 5\Topic A**.

Here's how	Here's why
1 Choose **Site, New Site...**	To open the Site Setup dialog box.
2 In the Site Name box, type **Outlander Links**	
3 Browse to the current topic folder	
Open the Outlander Spices folder, click **Select**, and click **Save**	To set the root folder for the site and create the site.
4 From the Files panel, open aboutus.html	
5 In the top navigation bar, double-click **Home**	To select it. You'll create a link that navigates to the home page.
6 In the Property inspector, click **HTML**	(If necessary.) To display the HTML options.
ACA objectives 4.5b, 4.5c In the Link box, enter **index.html**	To make the text "Home" a link to index.html. The file is in the same folder as the current page, so you don't need to specify the path.
Deselect the Home link	(Click anywhere on the page.) By default, links appear as blue, underlined text to distinguish link text from normal text. You can use CSS to customize link styles.
7 Save aboutus.html	
8 Open index.html	(From the Files panel.) You'll create a link on this page.

9	Triple-click **About Us**	To select the text.
10	Make "About Us" a link to aboutus.html	In the Property inspector, enter aboutus.html in the Link box.
	Save index.html	
11	Preview the page in your browser	(Press F12.) To see the link in action.
	Click **About Us**	The browser navigates to aboutus.html.
12	Click **Home**	The browser navigates to index.html.
	Close the browser	

Named anchors

Explanation

By using *named anchors*, you can mark an element on a page as a target, and then create a link that navigates directly to that target. This technique is often used to make it easier to jump to specific sections on long pages. You can also link to a named anchor on another page in your site to take the user directly to specific content.

ACA objectives 4.5a, 4.5f

To create a named anchor:

1. From the Visual Aids list, select Invisible Elements (if it's not already active, as indicated by a checkmark) so that named anchor tags are displayed in the Document window.
2. Place the insertion point at the target location.
3. In the Insert panel, click the Named Anchor button to open the Named Anchor dialog box.
4. In the Anchor Name box, type a name for the anchor.
5. Click OK.

To link to a named anchor, select the text or image that will serve as the link. Then, in the Property inspector, do one of the following:

- In the Link box, type # (the number sign), followed immediately by the name of the anchor. For example: #*anchorName*.
- Drag the Point-to-File icon to the named anchor.

Do it!

A-2: Creating and linking to a named anchor

Here's how	Here's why
1 Switch to aboutus.html	
2 On the Document toolbar, click [eye icon]	To display the Visual Aids list.
Verify that Invisible Elements is active	(There should be a checkmark next to it.) This visual aid will display symbols for named anchors.
3 Switch to Code view	You'll add an anchor at the top of the document. Switching to Code view sometimes makes it easier to place the insertion point in a precise location in the document structure.
Click to the right of <body>	``` </head> <body> ```
	At the top of the source code.
4 In the Insert panel, click [anchor icon]	(The Named Anchor button.) The Named Anchor dialog box appears.
In the Anchor Name box, type **top**	You'll create a link to this location in the document.
Click **OK**	(Or press Enter.) To insert the anchor.
5 Switch to Design view	
Deselect the anchor	[anchor icon image]
	(Click anywhere on the page.) To see the Named Anchor icon. This icon will not appear in a browser—it's displayed only in Design view.
6 Scroll to the bottom of the page and select the text **Go to Top**	You'll make this text a link to the *top* anchor.
In the Property inspector, in the Link box, enter **#top**	Links to named anchors start with the # sign.

Tell students that they're switching to code view here so that they can insert the anchor at the very top of the page. Sometimes it's hard to select specific areas of a document in Design view.

TIPS *Students can also choose Insert, Named Anchor or press Ctrl+Alt+A.*

ACA objective 4.5f

7	Click at the start of the "Our Spices" heading	To place the insertion point.
	In the Insert panel, click	
	Type **spices** and click **OK**	To create an anchor next to the heading.
8	Insert a named anchor next to the "Expansion Project" heading	
	Type **expansion** and click **OK**	
9	At the top of the page, select **Our Spices**	(In the navigation bar.) You'll make this a link to the "Our Spices" section.
	Create a link to the Spices anchor	In the Link box, type #spices.
10	Make "Expansion Project" a link to the other named anchor	
11	Save aboutus.html	
12	Preview the page in your browser	Press F12.
	Click **Our Spices**	To go to the Our Spices heading on the page.
	Click the Back button in your browser	
	Click **Expansion Project**	To go to the Expansion Project heading.
	Click **Go to Top**	To go back to the top of the page.
13	Close the browser	

Point out that the browser can go only as low as the bottom of the page, so the heading might not be displayed at the top of the page.

External links and e-mail links

Explanation

ACA objective 4.5a

External links navigate to a page or resource on another Web site. To create an external link, you need to specify the complete address of the destination page or resource. You can also create an *e-mail link*, which starts the user's default e-mail program, begins an outgoing message, and inserts the specified e-mail address in the To field.

To create an external link:

1 Select the text or image that you want to serve as the link.

ACA objective 4.5d

2 In the Property inspector, in the Link box, type the complete URL of the destination page or resource.

ACA objective 4.5e

To create an e-mail link:

1 Select the text or image that you want to serve as the link.

2 In the Property inspector, in the Link box, type `mailto:` followed by the recipient's e-mail address.

Absolute paths

ACA objective 4.5b

An *absolute path* is the complete URL for a file, including the Internet protocol to use (typically `http://` or `https://` for Web pages). For example, the address `http://www.outlanderspices.com/products/spices.html` is an absolute path to the file spices.html. When you link to an external resource, use an absolute path.

Link targets

ACA objective 4.5g

You can control how a link is opened in a browser. For example, you can set a link to open in a new browser window by specifying `_blank` as the link's target. Link targets are typically needed in framed Web pages and pop-up windows.

To specify a link target, select the text or image that serves as the link. Then, in the Property inspector, select an option from the Target list.

Do it!

A-3: Creating external links and e-mail links

Here's how	Here's why
1 Switch to index.html	
2 Select the ISO 9000 award image	(Near the bottom of the page.) You'll make this image an external link.

Outlander Spices has been awarded an ISO 9000 certification. Students will add a link to the iso.org Web site.

ACA objectives 4.5b, 4.5d

Here's how	Here's why
3 In the Link box, enter **http://www.iso.org**	In the Property inspector.
Deselect the image	There's a blue border around the image. By default, some browsers draw a blue border around images that are links. This is usually an undesired effect, so you'll disable the border.

	4 Select the image again	
	In the Border box, enter **0**	(In the Property inspector.) To remove the default border.
	Deselect the image	To verify that the blue border is gone.
	5 At the top of the page, select **Contact**	You'll make this text an e-mail link.
ACA objective 4.5e	In the Link box, enter **mailto:info@outlanderspices.com**	
		When the user clicks the link, his or her default e-mail program will open, with this address used for the outgoing message.
	6 Save index.html	
	Preview the page in your browser	
If the Outlook Express Wizard opens, tell students to click Cancel. A New Message window will then open.	7 Click **Contact**	An e-mail message with the specified address opens in the default e-mail application. (If no e-mail application is configured on the computer, you're prompted to configure one.)
If students are using a different browser, they can skip this step.	Click **Allow**	(If necessary.) To close the Internet Explorer Security dialog box.
	Close the e-mail message	(If applicable.) Do not save the message.
	8 Click the ISO 9000 award image	To go to the ISO Web site.
	Close the browser	
	9 In Dreamweaver, click the ISO 9000 image again	To select it.
ACA objective 4.5g	From the Target box, select **_blank**	
	Save your changes	
	10 Preview the page in your browser	
	Click the ISO 9000 award image	To go to the ISO Web site. This time, the page opens in a new browser window.
	Close both browser windows	
	11 Close index.html	

Image maps

Explanation

ACA objective 4.8a

An *image map* is an image that contains multiple links. Areas within the image, called *hotspots*, are links to other pages, resources, or named anchors. Image maps provide a unique, interactive design tool that you can use in a variety of design contexts.

Defining hotspots

A *hotspot* in an image map can be any size and any one of several shapes: oval, circle, rectangle, square, or irregularly shaped polygon.

ACA objectives 4.8b, 4.8d

To create an image map:

1 Select the image in the Document window. If necessary, expand the Property inspector by clicking the triangle in the lower-right corner.

2 In the Property inspector, in the Map box, enter a unique name for the image map.

3 Click the Rectangular Hotspot Tool, the Oval Hotspot Tool, or the Polygon Hotspot Tool.

4 Drag to draw the outline, or if you're using the Polygon tool, click the corners of the shape to begin the outline.

5 Use the Point-to-File icon or the Browse for File button to create a local link, a named anchor, or an external link.

Specifying Alt text for each hotspot

ACA objective 4.8c

In an image map, it's important to provide alternate (Alt) text for the image itself, as well as for each hotspot. Screen readers will be able to read the Alt text for the hotspots in the order in which they appear in the code. Without the Alt text for each hotspot, screen readers will read each entire link address, which can be long and unhelpful to the user of that device. You enter alternate text for a hotspot in the Alt box in the Property inspector.

Do it!

A-4:   Creating an image map

Here's how	Here's why
1 Open locations.html	From the Files panel. The page contains several named anchors. You'll create links to them in an image map.
Click the image of the U.S.	To select it.
2 In the Property inspector, in the Map box, enter **locations**	To name the map.
3 Click [□]	(The Rectangular Hotspot Tool is in the Property inspector.) You'll draw a hotspot.

ACA objectives 4.8a, 4.8b

Tell students to point to the upper-left corner of the image of the state of Oregon.	4 Point to **OR**, as shown	

(The pointer changes to a crosshair.) You'll insert a hotspot here. When a user clicks the image of Oregon, the browser will go to the specified destination.

Drag over and down to draw a rectangle, as shown

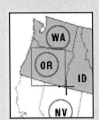

This defines the clickable region for this link. A dialog box appears, reminding you to describe this hotspot for users with alternative devices.

Click **OK**

ACA objectives 4.8c, 4.8d

5 In the Alt box, type **Oregon**

To provide alternate text for users with screen readers and similar devices.

6 Edit the Link box to read **#Oregon**

Link   #Oregon

Press ↵ ENTER

To create a link from the hotspot to the Oregon anchor.

Facilitate a brief discussion.

7 Is the Rectangular Hotspot Tool the most appropriate tool for this hotspot?

Why or why not?

Answers may vary. The Rectangular Hotspot Tool is best for rectangles. Most of the states aren't rectangles, so it's impossible to create a hotspot around an entire state without touching other states. In this case, the Polygon Hotspot Tool would be more effective.

8 Click

(The Polygon Hotspot Tool is in the Property inspector.) You'll create a polygon hotspot.

Help students create the polygon hotspot, if necessary.

9 Point to **NV**, as shown

The pointer changes to a crosshair.

10 Click the top-right corner of the state border, as shown

To set the first point of the hotspot polygon. The dialog box opens, reminding you to provide alternate text for the hotspot.

Click **OK**

11 In the Alt box, type **Nevada**

Click the top-left corner of the state border, as shown

To define the second point of the polygon. A line appears between the two points.

Students' hotspots might not be the exact same shape, but make sure that the hotspot for Oregon doesn't overlap the one for Nevada.

12 Continue clicking each corner until the hotspot takes the shape of the state, as shown

13 Create a link to the named anchor **#Nevada**

Edit the Link box to read #Nevada.

14 Save locations.html

Preview the page in your browser

15 Click **OR**

To navigate to the Oregon anchor.

Scroll up to display the map

If necessary.

Tell students that the vertical size of the browser window might determine whether the target region is displayed at the very top of the browser window.

Click **NV**

To navigate to the Nevada anchor. If the Nevada anchor is not displayed at the top of the browser window, the browser window is not large enough vertically. You can see the intended result if you decrease the vertical size of the browser.

16 Close the browser, and then close locations.html

Topic B: Applying link styles

This topic covers the following Adobe ACA exam objectives for Dreamweaver CS5.

#	Objective
5.1b	Demonstrate knowledge of how to set or modify global page properties and global CSS styles, including those for text, links, and backgrounds.
5.3b	Demonstrate knowledge of how to change the font, font size, and color.
5.8b	Demonstrate knowledge of how to use CSS to set properties for text and HTML tags.
5.8e	Demonstrate knowledge of how to use different selector types, such as descendent selectors, classes, tag selectors, pseudo class selectors, and group selectors.

Link states

Explanation

By default, text links appear as blue, underlined text. These default styles might not work within your site's color scheme. You can apply CSS styles to links to customize their appearance in a variety of ways. You can also assign styles that act as visual cues to the state of a link. *Link states* define the current condition of a link.

There are four link states, as described in the following table.

State	Description
Link	The default state of a link that hasn't been activated in any way.
Visited	The state of a link after you click it and its destination page has loaded. In many browsers, visited links appear as purple, underlined text by default.
Hover	The state of a link when you point to it. Most browsers don't apply any default formatting to the hover state.
Active	The state of a link when you click it but haven't yet released the mouse button. A link is in this state for only a moment.

Visited links

The browser's cache keeps track of links whose destinations have been viewed. When a link has been visited, the link remains in that state until the browser's cache is cleared. If you recently viewed the page that a link references, the link often appears in the visited state even if you didn't click it.

Creating link styles

ACA objectives 5.1b, 5.8e

To apply styles that target link states, you use *compound selectors* (also called *pseudo class selectors*). These are similar to class selectors but use a different syntax to specifically target the various states of a hyperlink. You can create these styles manually in a style sheet, or you can let Dreamweaver write the code, as follows:

1 In the CSS Styles panel, click the New CSS Rule button.

2 From the Selector Type list, select Compound.

3 From the Selector Name list, select either a:link, a:hover, a:visited, or a:active, depending on the link state for which you're defining a style. (You can also type a value in the box.)

4 In the Rule Definition list, select the style sheet (if necessary), and then click OK.

5 Set the desired styles and click OK.

Do it!

B-1: Applying styles to link states

The files for this activity are in Student Data folder **Unit 5\Topic B**.

Here's how	Here's why
1 Choose **Site, New Site...**	To open the Site Setup dialog box.
2 In the Site Name box, type **Outlander Styles**	
3 Browse to the current topic folder	
Open the Outlander Spices folder, click **Select**, and click **Save**	To set the root folder for the site and create the site.
4 Open index.html	
Observe the links in the navigation bar	The links are blue and underlined. This is the default formatting that most browsers apply to links. Blue text doesn't fit with this site's color scheme, and it strains the eyes against the green background color.
5 Collapse the Insert panel	To make more room for the CSS Styles panel.
6 Expand the CSS Styles panel	If necessary.
Click	To open the New CSS Rule dialog box.
ACA objective 5.1b 7 From the Selector Type list, select **Compound**	
ACA objective 5.8e From the Selector Name list, select **a:link**	
In the Rule Definition list, verify that **globalstyles.css** is selected	

	8 Click **OK**	To create a style for the default link state. The CSS Rule Definition dialog box appears.
ACA objectives 5.3b, 5.8b	9 From the Font-weight list, select **bold**	
	Click the Color box and select the dark green color **#030**	In the top row of the color picker.
	Under text-decoration, check **none**	To remove the default underline.
	Click **OK**	To format this link state and close the dialog box. The Home link shows the formatting you specified.
ACA objective 5.8e	10 Create a CSS rule for **a:visited**	Click the New CSS Rule button in the CSS panel. In the New CSS Rule dialog box, select a:visited from the Selector list, and click OK.
TIPS ✓ *Tell students that they can select this color from the vertical bar of colors on the left side of the color picker.*	Make the text black	(The value is #000.) Click the Color box and select the black color swatch in the upper-left corner.
	Make the text bold	From the Font-weight list, select bold.
	Under text-decoration, check **none**	To remove the default underline for the visited state.
	Click **OK**	
ACA objective 5.8e	11 Create a CSS rule for **a:hover**	
	Make the text bold and white	
	12 Open globalstyles.css	On the Related Files toolbar, click globalstyles.css.
	Press `CTRL` + `S`	To save the style sheet with the changes you made.
	13 Preview the page in your browser	Press F12.
	Observe the links	The links you have visited have the color you applied to the a:visited rule.
	14 Point to the links	The link text changes to white.
	15 Close the browser	
	Save and close all files	

Unit summary: Links

Topic A   In this topic, you learned how to **create links** to pages within a Web site, and you created named anchors and linked to them. You also learned how to create external links and e-mail links. You then learned how to create an **image map**. You learned how to draw **hotspots** on an image map with various shape tools and link those hotspots to other destinations.

Topic B   In this topic, you learned how to apply CSS styles to **link states**. You learned that applying link styles creates visual cues about the status of links on a page and allows you to fit your links into your color scheme.

Independent practice activity

In this activity, you'll create external links, an e-mail link, and an image map. Then you'll create named anchors, link to them, and apply link styles.

The files for this activity are in Student Data folder **Unit 5\Unit summary**.

1 Define a new site named **Practice Links**, using the Outlander Spices folder as the site's root directory.

2 Open index.html.

3 For the Home, About Us, Locations, and Contact items in the navigation bar, create links to their corresponding Web pages. For Contact, specify a link to the e-mail address **contact@outlanderspices.com**.

4 Apply link styles of your choice to the links, using the **a:link**, **a:visited**, and **a:hover** selectors.

5 Save your changes and test the links in your browser. Then close the browser and close index.html.

6 Open locations.html.

7 Insert named anchors next to the Washington and California rows in the table.

8 Create polygon hotspots for Washington and California. Specify alternate text for each hotspot, and then link the hotspots to their corresponding anchors.

9 Save locations.html and test the links in your browser.

10 Close the browser and any open files.

Review questions

1 To create a link to a location within a document, you need to:

A Create a local link on a page.

B Create a named anchor and then link to that anchor.

C Create a link from one anchor to another.

D Create a link to a page, and then on that page, create a link back to the original page.

2 The default link state is defined by which selector?

A a:active

B a:link

C a:visited

D a:hover

3 The active state is:

A The default state of a link.

B The state a link enters when you click it.

C The state a link enters when you point to it.

D The state a link enters when it has already been clicked.

4 The hover state is:

A The default state of a link.

B The state a link enters when you click it.

C The state a link enters when you point to it.

D The state a link enters when it has already been clicked.

5 True or false? To make an image map accessible to users with assistive devices like screen readers, you just have to specify alternate text for the image itself.

False. You should provide alternate text for the image itself, as well as for each hotspot.

Unit 6

Image formats and attributes

Unit time: 25 minutes

Complete this unit, and you'll know how to:

A Choose appropriate image formats, insert images and modify image properties, write effective alternate text, and insert and modify background images.

Topic A: Working with images

This topic covers the following Adobe ACA exam objectives for Dreamweaver CS5.

#	Objective
1.5b	Identify page elements that are affected by end-user technical factors such as download speed, screen resolution, operating system, and browser type.
2.3a	Demonstrate knowledge of graphic design elements and principles.
2.3c	Recognize examples of page designs that violate design principles or best practices.
2.4c	Identify specific techniques used to make a website accessible to viewers with visual and motor impairments.
2.4d	Identify elements of a website that by default are not read by screen readers.
4.4a	Demonstrate knowledge of the steps for inserting images.
4.4b	Demonstrate knowledge of how to add alternative text to images by using the Image Tag Accessibility Attributes dialog box or the Property inspector.
4.4c	Identify image file types that can be viewed in all browsers.
4.4d	Demonstrate knowledge of image file types and their uses.
5.1b	Demonstrate knowledge of how to set or modify global page properties and global CSS styles, including those for text, links, and backgrounds.
5.6a	Demonstrate knowledge of HTML tags.

Images on the Web

Explanation

Images are an integral part of Web design. They catch the user's eye, they can introduce a unique artistic aspect to site designs, and they can often deliver information in a way that text can't. For example, images of products give potential buyers visual information that can't be matched by a text description.

ACA objective 1.5b

File size is a vital consideration when you use images on Web pages. Large image files can take a long time to load in a user's browser. Try to keep your image file sizes as small as possible without sacrificing quality.

File formats

ACA objectives 4.4c, 4.4d

The three main image formats supported by Web browsers are GIF, JPEG, and PNG. GIF images, which can contain a maximum of 256 colors, are best used for images with relatively few colors and with areas of flat color, such as line drawings, logos, and illustrations. GIFs also support animation and transparency. The GIF format isn't recommended for photographs or illustrations with complex color gradations. When you save simple images with fewer than 256 colors, GIF uses a *lossless* compression algorithm, which means that no image data is discarded to compress the image.

The JPEG format supports more than 16 million colors, so it's best for photographs and images that have many subtle color shadings. JPEG uses *lossy* compression, which means that some image data is discarded when the file is saved.

The PNG format combines some of the best features of JPEG and GIF. It supports more than 16 million colors, so it's ideal for photos and complex drawings. It can use a variety of lossless compression algorithms, and it supports many levels of transparency, allowing areas of an image to appear transparent or semitransparent.

The following table summarizes these three image file formats.

	GIF	JPEG	PNG
Best used for:	Simple images with few colors	Photographs	Photographs or simple images
Maximum colors	256	More than 16 million	More than 16 million
Compression	Lossless	Lossy	Lossless
Transparency	One level (complete transparency)	Not supported	Multiple levels

Do it!

A-1: Discussing image formats

Facilitate a brief discussion.

ACA objective 4.4d

ACA objective 1.5b

Questions	Answers
1 Which image formats are typically best for photographs?	*JPEG and PNG.*
2 Which image formats support transparency?	*GIF and PNG.*
3 True or false: The GIF format and the JPEG format support the same number of colors.	*False. The GIF format can support up to 256 colors, and the JPEG format can support millions of colors.*
4 A corporate logo that contains text and six colors is probably best saved in which image format?	*GIF.*
5 Why is it important to limit the file size of your images?	*Images with large file sizes increase the total page size, or "page weight," causing pages to load slowly. Even if your images are small, using too many images on a single page can result in slow download times.*

Image-based text

Explanation

You can add text to a page in the form of an image. If you have a graphics application, such as Adobe Photoshop, Adobe Illustrator, or Adobe Fireworks, you can create text in a graphics file and save it with the appropriate file extension (typically .gif or .png). Image-based text is often used for logos or headings that require special styling that can't be achieved with HTML or CSS.

Advantages

By using image-based text, you can take advantage of exotic fonts that visitors aren't likely to have on their machines and would therefore be unable to display. You can also apply special effects, such as color gradients or embossing.

Disadvantages

ACA objective 2.4c

Image-based text has its disadvantages. Using several images on a page increases the page weight and download time. Also, because the images aren't text, the content isn't searchable by search engines or by the browser's Find function. You can minimize this limitation by always providing effective alternate text for your images. For image-based text, your alternate text should duplicate the text in the image.

Do it!

A-2: Using images for text

Here's how	Here's why
1 Choose **Site, New Site...**	To open the Site Setup dialog box.
2 In the Site Name box, type **Outlander images**	
3 Browse to the current topic folder	
Open the Outlander Spices folder, click **Select**, and click **Save**	To set the root folder for this site and create the site.
4 Open recipes.html	(From the Files panel.) You'll replace the title of each recipe with an image that uses a script font. When you want to use unusual fonts in your design, you often need to use images.
5 Delete **Princely Potatoes**	Select the text and press Delete.
Expand the images folder	
6 Drag **heading-potatoes.gif** to the location of the deleted text	(From the images folder.) The Image Tag Accessibility Attributes dialog box appears.
In the Alternate text box, type **Princely Potatoes**	To give this image alternate text that matches the image's content so that screen readers can access the content and search engines can index the text.
Click **OK**	To insert the image as the recipe heading.

If not all of the files in the Files panel are visible, tell students to maximize its size by collapsing other panels.

ACA objective 4.4a

ACA objectives 2.4c, 4.4b

7 Delete **Outlander Chicken**

Make heading-chicken.gif the new heading	Drag the image above the recipe, on the same line as the Princely Potatoes heading. Type "Outlander Chicken" in the Alternate text box, and click OK.

8 Save your changes

Image attributes

Explanation

ACA objective 5.6a

When you drag an image onto a page, Dreamweaver writes the HTML code required to embed the image. This code consists of the image tag (`<img>`) and several attributes, which are properties for the element. The location of the `<img>` tag tells the browser where to embed the file, and the `src` attribute tells the browser where to find the image file. You can set image attributes by using the Property inspector.

The attributes of the `<img>` tag are described in the following table.

Attribute	Use	Description
src	Required	Specifies the path to the image file.
alt	Recommended	Provides alternate text. If the browser can't display the image, alternate text provides access to the text in the image or a description of the image, whichever is more appropriate.
height	Recommended	Specifies the height of the image.
width	Recommended	Specifies the width of the image.
vspace	Optional	Applies additional space on both vertical sides of the image (the top and bottom).
hspace	Optional	Applies additional space on both horizontal sides of the image (the left and right).
align	Optional	Aligns an image with text on the same line.
border	Optional	Specifies the pixel width of the border around an image that acts as a link.

Images and accessibility

ACA objectives 2.4c, 2.4d, 4.4b

You already know how to provide alternate text ("Alt" text) when you insert images. It's also important to understand the *reasons* that it's important to do so and to create meaningful and effective Alt text.

Many Internet users need to use alternative browsing software such as screen readers and Braille devices. For example, people who have visual impairments can browse Web content with screen readers, which read aloud the text content of a Web page but cannot describe an image. It's up to you, the developer, to describe what the user can't see. Depending on the nature of the image, there are several types of Alt text you can write.

Descriptive and instructive Alt text

Suppose that your page has two images that act as "previous" and "next" links to navigate through an online help system. If these images do not have Alt text, and a user with a screen reader tries to use this help system, the user is likely to get lost or confused. The user would have no idea that the images are a means of navigation, and the help system wouldn't be particularly helpful.

Also, screen readers read aloud any text inside a link, but if an image *is* a link, there's no text to read aloud. In this case, you would want to specify either descriptive or instructive text for the images. For example, "Previous page" would describe the purpose of the image. "Click to view the previous page" would provide instructions.

Descriptive text should describe the content of an image. For example, if you have a picture of an ocean view, your alternate text might be something like "Photo of an ocean view from the beach" or "View from Virginia Beach." Screen readers typically identify an image before reading its alt text. For example, it will say "Image—View from Virginia Beach."

Instructive text should clearly indicate an action that the user can or should take. Examples of instructive text include "Enter a plain-text version of this Web site" and "Click to disable sound."

Replacement text

Use *replacement text* when your image contains text that you want the user to read. For example, if you have a GIF image that displays the text "BeeHive Record Company," your Alt text should literally replace this content—it should read "BeeHive Record Company." You applied replacement text in the preceding activity.

Use proper punctuation in your Alt text

If your Alt text is a complete sentence or is made up of multiple sentences, you should always use proper punctuation. Screen readers use punctuation to emulate the natural pauses and inflections in speech.

Do it!

A-3: Setting image attributes

Here's how	Here's why
1 Select the image shown	
	You'll specify alternate text for this image.
In the Alt box, enter **Princely Potatoes recipe**	(In the Property inspector.) In this case, it's best to provide a brief description of the image. Screen readers typically identify an image as such before reading the text alternative.
2 In the V Space box, enter **10**	To add 10 pixels of space above and below the image.
3 Provide appropriate alternate text for the other recipe image	Select the image and enter a description in the Alt box in the Property inspector.
4 Give the image 10 pixels of vertical space	
5 Save the page and preview it in your browser	
Close the browser	

This activity is designed to emphasize the importance of alternate text.

ACA objective 4.4b

Facilitate a brief discussion with student volunteers.

ACA objective 2.4c

6 An image of an arrow and the word "download" is intended to prompt users to download a file. What type of alternate text is probably best for this image, and what text would you use?

Answers may vary. Replacement text for "download" may suffice, or instructive text, such as "Click to download the file," might be more effective.

7 Suppose you have an image that shows the application window of a new software program. What type of alternate text is probably best for this image, and what text would you use?

Answers may vary. Descriptive text is probably the most appropriate because the image is not a link and you want users to understand the image's content. Appropriate text might be "This image shows the application window."

Background images

Explanation

You can use an image as a background for an element, such as a table, or for an entire Web page. By default, background images repeat across and downward to occupy an element's entire dimensions. This repetition is called *tiling*. If the image of peppers shown in Exhibit 6-1 is inserted as a background for a table, the image will tile to fill the width and height of the table, as shown in Exhibit 6-2. If you're working with a background image for a page, the image might tile several times to occupy the space, depending on the size of the image relative to the size of the browser window.

ACA objectives 2.3a, 2.3c

Choose a background image that doesn't detract from the foreground of the page or make the text difficult to read. For example, the descriptions and prices in Exhibit 6-2 are difficult to read against the underlying peppers.

With CSS, you can prevent an image from tiling so that it appears only once. You can also specify that the image tiles only horizontally or only vertically.

Exhibit 6-1: A sample background image

ACA objective 2.3c

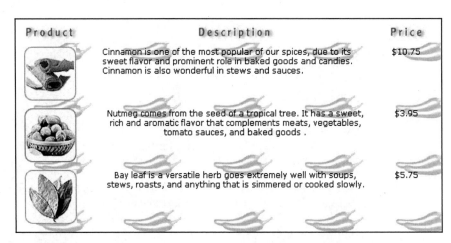

Exhibit 6-2: A small image used as a table background, tiling in both directions

Applying a background image to a page

You can apply a background image to a page and control how the image tiles by using the Page Properties dialog box. The Repeat list in this dialog box contains four options:

Repeat option	Description
no-repeat	Prevents the background image from tiling.
repeat	Tiles the background image both horizontally and vertically. This is the default behavior of background images.
repeat-x	Tiles the background image horizontally.
repeat-y	Tiles the background image vertically.

To apply a background image to the current page:
1   Choose Modify, Page Properties (or press Ctrl+J).
2   In the Category list, select Appearance (CSS).
3   Click Browse, navigate to the background image file, and click OK.
4   From the Repeat list, select an option. Click OK.

Applying a global page background

ACA objective 5.1b

If you want to create a global page background (one that applies to all pages linked to the same style sheet), create a rule for the `<body>` element in an external style sheet and set the desired background-image styles.

Applying a background image to an element

You can create a CSS rule that sets a background image, and then apply that rule to a specific element, such as a table or paragraph. The CSS Rule Definition dialog box contains additional options for controlling the appearance of a background image, as described in the following table.

Property	Description
Background-position (X)	Sets the horizontal position of the background image: left, center, right, or an integer value that you specify.
Background-position (Y)	Sets the vertical position of the background image: top, center, bottom, or an integer value that you specify.
Background-attachment	Determines whether the background image scrolls with the page content. Options include fixed and scroll (the default setting).

ACA objective 4.4a

To create and apply a background image by using a class style:
1   In the CSS Styles panel, click the New CSS Rule button.
2   Under Selector Type, select Class.
3   In the Selector Name box, type a class selector name. Click OK.
4   In the CSS Rule Definition dialog box, in the Category list, select Background.
5   Set the desired options and click OK.
6   Select the element to which you want to apply the background image. From the Class list in the Property inspector, select the class name.

Do it!

A-4: Inserting and controlling a background image

Here's how	Here's why
1 Collapse the images folder	
2 Open index.html	
3 Expand the CSS Styles panel	If necessary.
4 In the CSS Styles panel, double-click **body**	To open the CSS Rule Definition dialog box. You'll edit the CSS rule for the `<body>` element by applying a background image.
5 In the Category list, select **Background**	To display the background style options.
6 Click **Browse...**	To open the Select Image Source dialog box.
Open the images folder	
Select **spicebg.jpg**	Scroll down.
Click **OK**	
7 From the Background-repeat list, select **no-repeat**	To prevent the background image from repeating, or "tiling."
8 From the Background-position (X) list, select **right**	To align the background image with the right side of the page.
9 From the Background-position (Y) list, select **bottom**	To align the background image with the bottom of the page.
Click **OK**	
10 Switch to the style sheet and save the changes	On the Related Files toolbar, click globalstyles.css; then press Ctrl+S.
11 Preview the page in your browser, and scroll down	To view the background image. It has a very low opacity to ensure that it doesn't detract from the readability of the text.
12 At the top of the page, click **About Us**	To go to the aboutus.html page.
Scroll down the page	Because the background-image style was applied in the global style sheet, every page shares the background image.
Close the browser	
13 Close all open files	

ACA objective 5.1b (row 4)

ACA objective 4.4a (row 6)

ACA objective 2.3a (row 11)

Unit summary: Image formats and attributes

Topic A

In this topic, you learned about the **GIF**, **JPEG**, and **PNG** image formats. You learned the advantages and disadvantages of using image-based text, and you learned the attributes of the image tag. Then you learned how to write effective **Alt text** for your images based on different situations. Finally, you learned how to apply **background images** and control their positioning and tiling.

Independent practice activity

In this activity, you'll replace text with images and apply a background image to a table.

The files for this activity are in Student Data folder **Unit 6\Unit summary**.

1 Define a new site named **Practice images**, using the Outlander Spices folder as the site's root directory.

2 Open aboutus.html.

3 Replace the "Our History" heading with ourHistory.gif. Provide appropriate alternate text for the image.

4 Replace the "Our Spices" heading with ourSpices.gif. Provide appropriate alternate text.

5 Save your changes in aboutus.html.

6 Create a CSS class rule named **navTable** that applies the background image **greenbar.gif**. Prevent the background image from tiling. (The greenbar.gif image is in the images folder.)

7 Apply the navTable class style to the table containing the navigation links.

8 Save your changes in the style sheet.

9 View the results in your browser. The background image is a green bar that gradually lightens toward its right side.

10 Close all open files.

Review questions

1 Which of the following are advantages of using image-based text? [Choose all that apply.]

   A Image-based text allows you to use exotic fonts and text effects.

   B Image-based text loads faster than normal text.

   c Image-based text can be more eye-catching than normal text.

   D Image-based text is easier to read than normal text.

2 Which of the following are disadvantages of using image-based text? [Choose all that apply.]

   A Too many images increase a page's overall size and download time.

   B The content in the image can't be indexed by search engines.

   C The alternate text you specify for the images can't be indexed by search engines.

   D Text in images is usually harder to read than actual text.

3 When your image contains text, your alternate text should:

   A Describe the content of the image.

   B Duplicate the text that appears in the image.

   C Be omitted.

   D Provide more information about the text.

4 Alternate text for a photograph without text should:

   A Briefly describe the content of the image.

   B Indicate that the image doesn't contain text.

   C Be omitted.

   D Indicate that it's a photographic image.

5 When you insert a background image, how is it tiled, by default?

   A Horizontally

   B Vertically

   c Horizontally and vertically

   D Diagonally

6 In the CSS Rule Definition dialog box, how can you align a non-repeating background image to the top of an element?

   A From the background-position (X) list, select top.

   B From the background-attachment list, select top.

   c From the background-position (Y) list, select top.

   D From the background-image list, select top.

U n i t   7
Publishing

Unit time: 45 minutes

Complete this unit, and you'll know how to:

A Recognize copyright issues; check file size, download times, and spelling; check for broken links and orphaned files; cloak files; connect to a Web server; and upload and update a site.

Topic A: Site checks and publishing

This topic covers the following Adobe ACA exam objectives for Dreamweaver CS5.

#	Objective
1.3a	Use copyright terms correctly, such as "copyrighted," "fair use doctrine," "intellectual property," and "derivative works."
1.3b	Identify when permission must be obtained to use copyrighted material.
1.3c	Identify methods used to indicate content as copyrighted.
1.3d	Recognize proper methods for citing websites, images, sounds, video, and text from the Internet.
1.5a	Demonstrate knowledge of the relationship between end-user requirements and design and development decisions.
4.1a	Demonstrate knowledge of the terms "local site," "remote site/folder," "Web server," and "root folder."
4.2c	Demonstrate knowledge of best practices for naming HTML files.
6.1a	Demonstrate knowledge of how to check spelling on a Web page.
6.1b	Demonstrate knowledge of how to test links by using the Check Links Sitewide command.
6.5d	Demonstrate knowledge of the terms "Get," Put," "Check In," "Check Out," "Publish," and "Remote Server" as they apply to managing files and publishing a website.
6.5e	Demonstrate knowledge of expanding and collapsing the Files panel to access features such as the site map, Get and Put, Check In and Check Out, and refreshing the Files panel.
6.5h	Demonstrate knowledge of FTP server and Web server relationships to a Dreamweaver site.
6.6a	Demonstrate knowledge of how to set up a connection to a remote server.
6.6b	Demonstrate knowledge of how to publish files to a remote server.
6.6c	Demonstrate knowledge of how to use the Files panel to connect to and disconnect from a remote site, how to upload files to a remote site, and how to download files from a remote site.

Copyrighted works

Explanation

The volume of images and text online makes it easier than ever to find material that you might want to use. However, it's critical that you are careful not to violate copyright laws. Before using any image or text from an online source, make sure you understand copyright restrictions and obtain permission to use the material.

ACA objective 1.3a

Copyright is a kind of *intellectual property*, a creation of the mind for which property rights are recognized. (Other kinds of intellectual property include trademarks, patents, and symbols.) Copyright law extends to a wide range of works, including books, photographs, drawings, and motion pictures. In general, though, copyright is designed to protect the *expression* of an idea (not the idea itself; just the particular expression of it).

ACA objective 1.3b

A work that is copyrighted is protected by law from being copied and used without the copyright holder's permission, whether or not the work has been published. Although copyright laws vary from country to country, they generally protect a work for the lifetime of the creator plus 50 to 70 years. In the United States, if the work was created on or after January 1, 1978, then it's protected for the creator's lifetime plus 70 years.

ACA objective 1.3c

Before 1989, a work was protected by copyright law only if the creator had obtained a copyright notice, indicated by the word "copyright" or the © symbol followed by the date of publication and the copyright owner's name. Since 1989, copyright protection has been extended automatically to the author of any work that has been created in a fixed form. One exception is a work for hire; in that situation, the employer retains the copyright.

Fair use and derivative works

ACA objective 1.3a

Even though it seems like copyright law protects nearly every work, there are some ways to avoid violating the law while making use of another's work. The doctrine of *fair use* extends to specific situations, such as criticism, news reporting, teaching, scholarship, and research, and it allows limited use of copyrighted material. The guidelines are still vague, however, and it should be noted that fair use doesn't include using the material as part of a profit-earning venture.

The doctrine of fair use has sometimes been used to defend situations involving *derivative works*, or works based on another work. Derivative works must be different enough from the original to be regarded as a "new work" in their own right, or they must contain a substantial amount of new material in addition to the original work. In short, the derivative work must itself be copyrightable.

Copyright permission and model releases

ACA objective 1.3b

You should always attempt to obtain permission from the copyright holder before using any copyrighted material, except in obvious cases of fair use. You should also be sure that the ownership is clear—sometimes, as with works for hire, the creator of the image might not be the copyright holder.

Another factor to consider is the use of recognizable people in images. If you publish an image (even one you've taken) of a recognizable subject without his or her permission, you could be subject to civil liability. The original photographer typically obtains permission by having the subject sign a *model release*, a legal document granting permission to publish someone's image.

Citing sources

ACA objective 1.3d

If you use copyrighted material in your site, be sure you first ask permission to use the material, and always give proper credit to the copyright holder, either at the point the material is used or by using a footnote. This guideline applies to any copyrighted material, whether it's text, audio, video, or artwork.

Do it!

A-1:   Discussing copyrighted works

Questions and answers

1   What legal protections extend to copyrighted works?

   A work that is copyrighted is protected by law from being copied and used without the copyright holder's permission, whether or not the work has been published.

2   Does a work need to have a visible copyright symbol in order to be protected by copyright law?

   No. Copyright protection extends automatically to the author of any work that has been created in a fixed form.

3   Can you cite the doctrine of fair use when reproducing an image you found online for use in your company's advertising?

   No. The doctrine of fair use extends to specific situations such as criticism, news reporting, teaching, scholarship, and research.

4   Discuss what works might be considered "derivative" of a copyrighted work.

   Students might discuss such things as translations, dramatizations or fictionalizations, or motion pictures based on books.

5   When do you need to obtain permission before using a copyrighted work?

   Always, except in clear cases of fair use.

6   You've obtained permission to use a photograph containing a family of four people. What else should you obtain before you publish the image?

   If the photograph contains recognizable people, you must obtain a model release before publishing the image.

Checking page size and download time

Explanation

Before you upload a site, it's important to verify that your page "weight" isn't excessive. *Page weight* is the total file size of a document and all the resources (images, movies, scripts, style sheets, etc.) that it loads when the page is requested by a visitor. The higher the page weight, the longer it takes to load the page. If your pages load slowly, some users (particularly those with slower connections) might leave your site and seek similar information or services elsewhere.

Dreamweaver calculates the size of an open document by counting up the kilobytes (K) of the document and all the resources that load along with it. The download time of a page at a particular connection speed is displayed in the status bar in the Document window.

Changing the download time baseline

By default, the connection speed in the status bar is set to 384K, which is a slow baseline by today's standards. You can change this setting in the Status Bar category in the Preferences dialog box. The default you set should be based on an analysis of your target audience.

Checking spelling

ACA objective 6.1a

It's also important that you check for spelling errors and typos before you publish a site. To check spelling on a page, choose Commands, Check Spelling (or press Shift+F7).

Do it!   ## A-2:   Checking page size, download time, and spelling

Here's how	Here's why
1 Open the Site Setup dialog box	
2 In the Site Name box, type **Publishing**	
3 Browse to the current topic folder	
Open the Outlander Spices folder, click **Select**, and click **Save**	To set the root folder for this site and create the site.
4 Open products.html	From the Files panel.
In the status bar, observe the page size and download time	This page's size is approximately 120K, and the page will take about 3 seconds to load. (This interval is based on the default assumption of a connection speed of approximately 384K.)
5 Choose **Edit**, **Preferences...**	To open the Preferences dialog box.
In the Category list, select **Status Bar**	To display status bar options.
From the Connection speed list, select **1500**	To set a faster connection speed as the target baseline. After conducting an audience analysis, you have determined that this is closer to the average speed with which your visitors access your site.
Click **OK**	To close the dialog box.
6 Check the download time again	For users connecting at an average of approximately 1500K, the page will download in about 1 second.
7 How might you use this feature to help you create a successful site?	*Answers may vary. If your target audience is likely to use slower connection speeds, you can use this information to determine if you should optimize your images or reduce the number of images used.*
8 Choose **Commands**, **Check Spelling**	To open the Spell Checking dialog box. The word "Panang" is not recognized.
Click **Ignore**	
Click **Yes**	(If necessary.) To keep checking from the beginning of the document.
Click **OK**	No spelling errors are found in this page.
9 Close products.html	

Tell students to expand the Files panel, if necessary.

TIPS *Students can also press Ctrl+U.*

Point out that students can select an option from the list or enter their own speed.

ACA objective 1.5a

TIPS *Sutdents can also press Shift+F7.*

ACA objective 6.1a

Broken links and orphaned files

Explanation

Before you publish a Web site, you should verify that all of the links in the site work correctly. As you build pages, it's often easy to mistype a link or accidentally link to a page that was later deleted or renamed. If users click a broken link, the browser will display an error message indicating that the linked page cannot be found. Having to open each file and test every link would be a time-consuming and tedious development task. Fortunately, Dreamweaver can check the integrity of all of your local and external links for you.

ACA objective 6.1b

To check links for an entire site:

1   Choose Site, Check Links Sitewide, or press Ctrl+F8. (You can also right-click in the Files panel and choose Check Links, Entire Local Site.) The Link Checker panel opens.

2   In the Link Checker panel, identify and repair broken links.

3   From the Show list, select External Links if you want to review the external links in the site.

4   From the Show list, select Orphaned Files to display any orphaned files that might exist in the site.

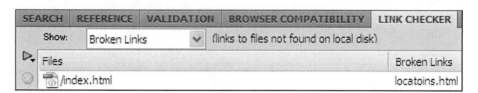

Exhibit 7-1: The Link Checker panel

Orphaned files

Orphaned files are files that reside in your site folders but have no pages linking to them. These files might include early drafts of Web pages or image files that you decided not to use. Removing orphaned files from your site before uploading prevents unnecessary bloat on the server and makes site maintenance easier. In the Link Checker panel, select Orphaned Files from the Show List.

Cloaking

Sometimes you might have orphaned files that you don't want to remove from the site. For example, you might have text documents or original image files, such as those in the Photoshop .psd format, that you might want to use later. Keeping them with the site folder makes them easier to find.

Cloaking folders or file types allows you to store them in your site, but prevents them from being included in normal site operations, such as link reports or uploading functions. To cloak a folder, right-click it and choose Cloaking, Cloak. Cloaked folders and documents appear with a red line through their icons, as shown in Exhibit 7-2.

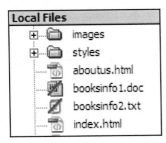

Exhibit 7-2: The Files panel, showing cloaked files

To cloak file types, right-click in the Files panel and choose Cloaking, Settings. In the Cloaking category in the Site Definition dialog box, check "Cloak files ending with" and then enter the file extensions you want to cloak.

Do it!

A-3:   Checking links and cloaking files

TIPS *Students can also press Ctrl+F8.*

ACA objective 6.1b

Here's how	Here's why
1 Choose **Site, Check Links Sitewide**	The Link Checker opens at the bottom of the Document window.
Observe the results	The list shows that one broken link was found on the index.html page. In this case, a typo in the file name breaks the link.
2 Under Broken Links, click **locatoins.html**	You'll correct the misspelling of the file name.
Type **locations.html**	To enter the correct file name for the linked file.
Press ⏎ ENTER	The file no longer appears in the list.
3 From the Show list, select **External Links**	To view the external links in this site's pages. These links don't indicate errors; they're listed for reference only.
4 From the Show list, select **Orphaned Files**	Several files appear that aren't linked to any pages in the site. You'll remove the image files. However, because you might need the text files later, you'll cloak those specific file types.
5 In the Files panel, expand the images folder	
Delete **spice_of_month.jpg** and **spicebg.jpg**	Select each file and press Delete.
Collapse the images subfolder	
6 Right-click in the Files panel and choose **Cloaking, Settings...**	To open the Site Setup for Publishing dialog box.
7 Check **Cloak files ending with**	

8 Edit the box to read **.doc .txt** as shown	☑ Cloak files ending with: .doc .txt|
Click **Save**	A dialog box appears, stating that the cache for the site will be re-created.
Click **OK** and observe the Files panel	The two documents now have a red line across their icons, indicating that the files are cloaked and won't be uploaded with the rest of the site. They also won't appear in the list of orphaned files.
9 Right-click **Link Checker**	(Or any other tab in the panel.) To display a shortcut menu.
Choose **Close Tab Group**	

Web site publishing

Explanation

ACA objective 4.1a

You publish a Web site by copying the site files from your local PC to a remote Web server. A *Web server* is a computer configured with Web server software and the Internet protocols required to serve pages and other resources upon request. Dreamweaver makes it easy to set publishing parameters for your site and to transfer your site files to a Web server.

A Web server is connected to the Internet via an *Internet service provider* (ISP) or a hosting center. The ISP or hosting center provides space for Web site files, as well as other services such as site promotion and search engine optimization.

File names

How you name your files can be important based on the type of server that is hosting the site. For example, sites hosted on a UNIX server may require different file path protocols than other servers. Ask your organization's IT personnel for guidance on file naming conventions.

ACA objective 4.2c

To create file names that comply with just about any operating system, follow these guidelines:

- Keep file names short. For ease of maintenance on the site, the file name should describe the file's content or function.
- Don't include spaces in the name. To separate words, use the underscore character; for example, *product_list.html*.
- Don't use any characters other than letters, numerals, and the underscore.
- Always start file names with a letter.
- Treat uppercase and lowercase letters as separate characters. For example, your server might not consider aboutus.html and AboutUs.html to be the same file. A good way to keep from running into problems is to use only lowercase letters.

Server connection methods

ACA objective 6.5h

Before you can upload your site files to a Web server, you must first establish a connection between your PC and the server. FTP (File Transfer Protocol) and SFTP (Secure File Transfer Protocol) are popular methods of transferring files. SFTP uses FTP, the standard file transfer protocol, and combines it with authentication and encryption protocols to protect the transmission.

WebDAV (Web-based Distributed Authoring and Versioning) is a set of extensions to the HTTP protocol that allow users to edit and manage files collaboratively on remote Web servers. Dreamweaver can also transfer data between servers located on a LAN (local area network), and transfer data by using Microsoft technologies such as the version control application VSS (Visual SourceSafe) and RDS (Remote Data Services).

Before setting up a server connection, check with your ISP or IT manager to make sure that the Web server supports the connection protocol you want to use. If it does, the ISP/IT manager typically provides the required information for connecting to the server, including the FTP host name, the host directory, and a login name and password.

Connecting to a remote server by using FTP

ACA objective 6.6a

To connect Dreamweaver to a remote server for publishing files:

1 Choose Site, Manage Sites to open the Manage Sites dialog box.
2 Select the site you want to configure and click Edit. The Site Setup dialog box opens.
3 Click Servers.
4 Click the Add New Server button.
5 Type the name of the server.
6 Verify that FTP is selected, and enter the address in the FTP Address box.
7 Enter your user name and password for the FTP server.
8 Specify the root directory for uploading the site.
9 Click Test to test the connection.
10 Click Save to save the connection. The server name appears in the Site Setup dialog box. You can manage multiple site connections from this dialog box.

Do it!

A-4: Using FTP to connect to a server

Students will simulate using SFTP to connect to a remote server.

Here's how	Here's why
1 Choose **Site, Manage Sites...**	To open the Manage Sites dialog box. You'll explore the settings for secure FTP connection.
2 Verify that **Publishing** is selected, and click **Edit**	The Site Setup dialog box opens. You'll explore the steps required to connect to a server through a secure FTP connection.
3 Click **Servers**	

ACA objective 6.5h

Read the dialog box	If one or more Web servers were configured, they would be listed here.

ACA objective 6.6a

4 Click ⊞	The Add New Server button is near the bottom of the dialog box.

Tell students that this is just a simulation of the process they would use.

Type **Outlander FTP Server**	(In the Server Name box.) If you're making a new connection, this is where you'll type the server name.
5 In the "Connect using" list, verify that **FTP** is selected	FTP is an abbreviation for File Transfer Protocol.

Tell students that this is a fictitious server address.

6 In the FTP Address box, type **ftp.OutlanderServer.com**	To specify the address of an FTP host where you will send files.
7 In the Username box, type your first name	In an actual situation, the server administrator would typically assign a user name.
In the Password box, type **password**	A server administrator would typically assign a password.
8 Observe the Root Directory folder	This is where you would specify the root directory for uploading the site.
9 Click **Cancel**	Normally, you would click Save and the server name would then appear in the list.
Click **Cancel**	To close the Site Setup dialog box.
Click **Done**	To close the Manage Sites dialog box.

Uploading a site

Explanation

ACA objective 6.5h

When you upload files to a Web server, the local folder on your PC (where the site files are stored) is automatically duplicated on the Web server. All files and subfolders are copied, except those that have cloaking applied to them. You can also publish a site to another location on your PC, either as a practice upload or if your PC is acting as the Web server or testing server.

ACA objective 6.5d

You upload files by using the Put File(s) button in the Files panel. With the "Put File(s)" command, you are literally "putting" the files on a remote server. When you download files from a remote server, you use the Get File(s) button in the Files panel—you're "getting" files from an outside source.

Expanding the Files panel

ACA objective 6.5e

After you have defined your remote server connection and connected to the server, you can expand the Files panel to display additional options for uploading a site, and to view both the local files and the remote folder you're publishing to.

Click the Expand/Collapse button in the Files panel to expand it. The window is then divided into the Remote Server pane on the left, and the Local Files pane on the right.

To upload a site to your remote server, you can use any of the following methods:

ACA objectives 6.6b, 6.6c

- To upload an entire site, select the root site folder and click the Put File(s) button.
- To upload a subfolder within the site, select the subfolder and click the Put File(s) button.
- To upload specific files, select the files and click the Put File(s) button.

In the expanded Files panel, you can also upload a site or individual files by dragging folders or files from the Local Files pane to their proper folders in the Remote Server pane.

Do it!

A-5: Uploading a site

Students will simulate publishing a site by "uploading" to another folder on their computer.

Here's how	Here's why
1 Open the Manage Sites dialog box	Choose Site, Manage Sites.
Verify that **Publishing** is selected	
Click **Edit**	You'll simulate uploading a site by transferring the site to a folder on your PC.
2 Click **Servers**	
Click ➕	
3 Type **Test Publish**	
ACA objective 6.6a 4 From the "Connect using" list, select **Local/Network**	Options related to Local/Network connections are displayed.

ACA objectives 6.5e, 6.6c

5 Next to Server Folder, click 🗁

Help students navigate to the Test Site folder, if necessary.

Navigate up one level, and open the Test Site folder

Click **Select** — To specify the Test Site folder as the remote folder. You'll simulate uploading a Web site.

6 Click **Save** — The server name appears in the list. Dreamweaver recognizes it as a remote server even though the destination folder resides on your PC.

Click **Save** — To close the Site Setup dialog box.

Click **Done** — To close the Manage Sites dialog box.

7 In the Files panel, click 🗗 — To expand the Files panel so that it shows the Local files pane on the right and the Remote Server pane on the left.

On the toolbar, click ↻ — (Or press F5.) To refresh the panel and display the remote folder. Because there's nothing in the folder yet, only the folder icon is displayed.

8 In the Local Files pane, select the Site folder — (The Site – Publishing folder.) You'll upload the entire site.

ACA objective 6.6b

Explain that this isn't a true upload because the files aren't being copied to a remote computer.

9 Click ⬆ — (The Put File(s) button.) To upload the site files from the local folder to the remote folder. A dialog box appears, asking if you're sure you want to put the entire site.

Click **OK** — To put (upload) the entire site to the "remote" folder.

Tell students that this is how it will look when they upload a Web site to an actual remote server.

Observe the folders in both panes — Both panes contain the same folders and files, except for the files you cloaked earlier.

10 Click 🗗 — (The Expand/Collapse button.) To collapse the Files panel.

Updating a site

Explanation

After you publish a site, you can still edit pages locally and then update the same files on the remote server. Depending on your organization's workflow procedures, you might want to first download the version of the file that's currently on the Web server. To do so, select the file(s) in the Remote Server pane of the expanded Files panel and then click the Get File(s) button. You might also want to get files from the remote server if you want to store multiple versions of the site in different folders.

ACA objective 6.6c

To download files from your Web server:

1 Connect to the remote site.

2 Download files or folders by using the following methods:

- To download an entire site, select the root site folder in the Remote Server pane of the expanded Files panel and then click the Get File(s) button.
- To download a specific file, select it in the Remote Server pane of the expanded Files panel and then click the Get File(s) button.

In the expanded Files panel, you can also drag folders or files from the Remote Server pane to their proper folders in the Local Files pane.

Dependent files

When you Get or Put a file, Dreamweaver prompts you to include that file's dependent files. *Dependent files* include assets and other files, such as images or style sheets, that are referenced by the file being put and that might have been altered or updated. To enable or disable this prompting, choose Edit, Preferences. Under Category, select Site. Then check or clear the Dependent files options.

Synchronization

Dreamweaver can synchronize your local and remote files by comparing the time stamps saved with each file. So, if you edit and save a page on the local site, it has a more recent time stamp than the version of that page on the server. To see which files are newer on the local site, right-click in the Files panel and choose Select, Newer Local. To see which files on the remote server are newer, choose Select, Newer Remote.

To synchronize the local and remote sites, do one of the following:

- Click the "Synchronize with (server name)" button.
- Right-click in the Files panel and choose Synchronize.
- Choose Site, Synchronize.

ACA objective 6.5d

Each of these commands opens the Synchronize Files dialog box, shown in Exhibit 7-3. Select synchronization options from the Synchronize and Direction lists, and click Preview. Dreamweaver then compares the time stamps of the two sites and updates the site containing the older files with the newer files. The Synchronize dialog box then appears, showing the file(s) that will be updated, and whether the action is a Put or Get. Click OK to complete the synchronization process.

Exhibit 7-3: The Synchronize Files dialog box

Do it!

A-6: Discussing site updates

Questions and answers

ACA objective 6.5d

1 What's a Get action?

A Get is the act of transferring a file, a folder, or an entire site from a remote server to your local computer. A Get is synonymous with downloading—you are copying files from a remote server to your local computer.

ACA objectives 6.6b, 6.6c

2 What's a Put action?

A Put is the reverse of a Get—it puts files on the remote server. A Put action is synonymous with uploading—you are copying files from a local machine to a remote server.

3 How does Dreamweaver help you manage related assets and files?

When you Get or Put files, Dreamweaver prompts you to include their dependent files, such as images and other assets.

4 How do you enable or disable dependent-file prompting?

Choose Edit, Preferences. In the Preferences dialog box, select the Site category. Check or clear the Dependent files options.

5 How can you easily ensure that your local site files and remote site files are the same and are the latest edited versions of the files?

By synchronizing your files. The Synchronize command compares the time stamps of the local site files and remote site files, and updates the site containing the older pages with the newer ones.

Unit summary: Publishing

Topic A

In this topic, you learned about **copyright issues** that are important to be aware of before publishing a site. Then you learned how to check the **file size** and download times for your pages, and check for and fix **broken links** and **orphaned files**. You also learned the basics of **Web site publishing** with Dreamweaver. You learned how to **connect to a server** using FTP, and you learned how to use the Files panel to upload a site to a remote server. Finally, you learned how to **synchronize** the local and remote versions of your site files, and download and upload site files by using the Get File(s) and Put File(s) buttons.

Independent practice activity

In this activity, you'll define a Web site, check for broken links and orphaned files, and practice uploading a Web site by uploading it to a local folder.

The files for this activity are in Student Data folder **Unit 7\Unit summary**.

1 Define a new Web site named **Practice Publishing**, using the Outlander Spices folder as the site's root directory.

2 Check the links in the site. (*Hint:* In the Files panel, right-click the site and choose Check Links, Entire Local Site.)

3 Repair the broken link that was caused by a typographic error.

4 Delete the orphaned files.

5 Establish a connection to the Test Site folder (in the Unit summary folder).

6 View both the local files and the "remote" Test Site folder. (*Hint:* Expand the Files panel.)

7 Upload the entire site to the Test Site folder. (*Hint:* In the Local Files pane, select the Site folder and then click the Put File(s) button.)

8 Collapse the Files panel, and close Dreamweaver.

Review questions

1 How can you change the connection speed with which Dreamweaver calculates download time?

   A Select a new connection speed from the Page size/download time list in the status bar.

   B Right-click the Page size/download time list in the status bar and choose a new connection speed.

   C Open the Page Properties dialog box, select the Title/Encoding category, and select a new connection speed from the Connection speed list.

   D Open the Preferences dialog box, select the Status Bar category, and select a new connection speed from the Connection speed list.

2 How can you check links site-wide? [Choose all that apply.]

   A Press Ctrl+F8.

   B Right-click the Files panel and choose Check Links, Entire Local Site.

   C Choose Site, Check Links Sitewide.

   D Select a file in the Files panel, and click Check Links Sitewide in the Property inspector.

3 How can you cloak specific file types?

   A In the Files panel, right-click a file that you want to cloak and choose Cloak File Type.

   B Open the Preferences dialog box and select the File Types/Editors category. Check "Cloak files ending with" and enter the file extensions you want to cloak.

   C Right-click the Files panel and choose Cloaking, Settings. In the Cloaking category, check "Cloak files ending with" and enter the file extensions you want to cloak.

   D Choose Site, Advanced, Cloak Files Ending With. In the dialog box, enter the file extensions you want to cloak.

4 Which of the following are general guidelines to consider when you're naming site files? [Choose all that apply.]

   A Keep file names as short and meaningful as possible.

   B Start file names with a number.

   C Start file names with a letter.

   D Don't include spaces in the file names.

   E Don't use special characters other than the underscore.

   F Separate words in the file names with one space only.

5 What legal protections extend to copyrighted works?

   A work that is copyrighted is protected by law from being copied and used without the copyright holder's permission, whether or not the work has been published.

6 When do you need to obtain permission before using a copyrighted work?

   Always, except in cases of fair use.

7 Which of the following are ways you can connect to a server? [Choose all that apply.]

A FTP

B SFTP

C XML

D WebDAV

8 How can you synchronize local and remote site files? [Choose all that apply.]

A Choose Site, Synchronize.

B In the Files panel, click the Refresh button.

C Choose File, Check Page, Check Accessibility.

D Right-click in the Files panel and choose Synchronize.

E Click the "Synchronize with (server name)" button.

9 After you connect to a remote server, how can you upload an individual file? [Choose all that apply.]

A Select the file in the Files panel and click the Put File(s) button.

B In the Files panel, select the folder containing the file and click the Put File(s) button.

C Expand the Files panel, and drag the folder containing the file from the Local Files pane to the Remote Site pane.

D Expand the Files panel, and drag the file from the Local Files pane to the appropriate folder in the Remote Server pane.

Course summary

This summary contains information to help you bring the course to a successful conclusion. Using this information, you'll be able to:

A Use the summary text to reinforce what students have learned in class.

B Direct students to the next courses in this series, if any, and to any other resources that might help students continue to learn about Dreamweaver CS5.

Topic A: Course summary

At the end of the class, use the following summary text to reinforce what students have learned. It is intended not as a script, but rather as a starting point.

Unit summaries

Unit 1

In this unit, students learned the basics of the Internet and HTML. Then they learned about basic principles of **project management**, effective communications management, and Web site planning. They identified the main components of the **Dreamweaver interface** and learned how to customize the **workspace**. Finally, students performed basic Web page editing by adding and formatting **text** and **images**, and they previewed a page in a browser.

Unit 2

In this unit, students learned some basic concepts about **planning a Web site** and using planning tools such as flowcharts, storyboards, and wireframes. Students also learned how to apply basic **design principles**. Then students defined a Web site and learned how to work with the **Files panel** and the Assets panel. Then they created Web pages, **imported text** from external documents, set **page properties**, identified basic HTML tags, switched between **document views**, worked with code and the **code tools**, inserted special characters, and used **Find and Replace** to update content.

Unit 3

In this unit, students learned how to define a basic **page structure** and how to create and modify **lists**. Students also learned how to create and attach **CSS style sheets**, define element styles, and create and apply class styles.

Unit 4

In this unit, students learned how to create and format **tables** and nested tables, write effective **table summaries**, insert rows and columns, and set row and column properties. Students also applied **fixed** and **variable widths** and modified cell borders and cell padding.

Unit 5

In this unit, students created **links** to other pages and resources and created **named anchors** and e-mail links. Then students created an **image map** and drew hotspots with various shape tools. Finally, students learned about the four **link states** and applied CSS styles to them.

Unit 6

In this unit, students learned about the GIF, JPEG, and PNG **image file formats**. Then students learned how to modify image properties and write effective **Alt text** depending on various circumstances. Finally, students learned how to insert **background images** and control their position and tiling.

Unit 7

In this unit, students learned how to recognize **copyright issues** and perform **site checks** before publishing a site. They learned how to check the file size and download times for site pages, and how to find and **fix broken links** and orphaned files. Finally, students learned how to cloak files, **connect to a remote server**, and upload and update a site.

Topic B: Continued learning after class

Point out to your students that it's impossible to learn to use any software effectively in a single day. To get the most out of this class, students should begin working with Dreamweaver CS5 to perform real tasks as soon as possible. We also offer resources for continued learning.

Next courses in this series

This is the first course in this series. The next course in this series is:

- *Dreamweaver CS5: Advanced, ACA Edition*

Other resources

For more information, visit www.axzopress.com.

Glossary

Assets

The components of your Web site, such as images and multimedia files.

Cell padding

The amount of space between a cell border and the cell content.

Class styles

CSS style rules that use class selectors, which allow you to give elements names that are relevant to your document structure. You can apply class styles to multiple elements on a page.

Definition list

An HTML list used for structuring terms and their corresponding definitions. Often used for glossaries, pages of frequently asked questions (FAQs), and similar contexts.

Deprecated tags

Tags that are discouraged in favor of newer, better options. For example, the `<font>` tag in older versions of HTML is now deprecated in favor of CSS.

Element styles

CSS style rules that use tag selectors to define the formatting of HTML elements, such as headings and paragraphs. An element style overrides any default formatting for an HTML element.

External links

Links to a page or resource outside a Web site.

External style sheet

A text file that is saved with a .css extension and that contains style rules that define how various HTML elements are displayed.

Font set

A group of similar typefaces that help ensure consistent text display in a variety of browsers and operating systems.

GIF

An image file format that can support a maximum of 256 colors. GIF files are best used for images with relatively few colors and with areas of flat color, such as line drawings, logos, and illustrations.

HTML

Hypertext Markup Language, the standard markup language on the Web. HTML consists of *tags* that define the basic structure of a Web page.

Image map

An image that contains multiple clickable regions called *hotspots*.

Internal links

Links to pages or resources within a Web site.

Internal style sheet

One or more style rules embedded in the head section of an HTML document. Styles in an internal style sheet affect elements in only that document.

Internet

A vast array of networks that belong to universities, businesses, organizations, governments, and individuals all over the world.

JPEG

An image file format that supports more than 16 million colors. JPEG is best used for photographs and images that have many subtle color shadings.

Link states

The four states, or conditions, that a link can be in: link, hover, active, and visited.

Margin

The space between page content and the edge of the browser window, or the space between individual elements.

Monospaced font

A typeface in which every character uses the same amount of space. For example, an "i" and an "m" take up the same amount of space on a line. Monospaced fonts, such as Courier, resemble typewriter text.

Named anchor

A code reference you can target as a link within a document. Named anchors are also called *bookmark links* or *intra-document links*.

Nested list

Also called a sub-list, a list that starts inside a list item tag of another list. Nested lists are used when you need to create indented sub-lists within a larger list.

Nested table

A table that's inserted in the cell of another table.

Nonbreaking space

A special HTML character that inserts a single space without breaking a line.

Ordered list

An HTML list structure that automatically appends sequential labels to each list item. By default, list items are numbered 1, 2, 3, and so on.

Orphaned files

Files that reside in your site folders but aren't linked to by any pages.

PNG

An image file format that combines some of the best features of JPEG and GIF. The PNG format supports more than 16 million colors and supports many levels of transparency. However, many older browsers don't fully support the PNG format.

Sans serif font

A typeface whose characters don't have serifs (flourishes or ornaments at the ends of the strokes that make up the letters).

Serif font

A typeface whose characters have serifs (flourishes or ornaments at the ends of the strokes that make up the letters).

Table cell

The intersection of a row and a column in a table. You insert content into table cells.

Unordered list

An HTML list structure that automatically appends bullets to each list item. Use this kind of list when the list items aren't sequential and don't need to be in any particular order.

Visual aids

Page icons, symbols, or borders that are visible only in Dreamweaver. You can turn certain visual aids on and off to make it easier to work with the page.

XHTML

Extensible Hypertext Markup Language, a strict version of HTML that doesn't allow proprietary tags or attributes. Instead, all style information is controlled by CSS. XHTML allows for cleaner, more efficient code. By default, Dreamweaver CS5 builds pages with XHTML code.

Index

A

Absolute paths, 5-8
Accessibility issues, 6-6
Alternate text, 1-30, 5-10, 6-6
AP Elements panel, 1-20
Application bar, 1-15
Assets panel, 1-20, 2-10
Audience, analyzing, 1-10

B

Background colors
    For pages, 2-20
    For rows, columns, and cells, 4-13
Background images, 6-8
Browsers, adding to Preview list, 1-32

C

Cells
    Changing width of, 4-13
    Padding vs. spacing, 4-18
    Selecting, 4-11
Class styles, 3-13
    Creating, 3-24
Cloaking, 7-7
Code Navigator, 2-24
Coding toolbar, 2-23
Colors
    Background, 2-20
    Hexadecimal notation for, 3-16
    Setting default for text, 2-20
    Specifying for rows, columns, and cells, 4-13
Columns
    Fixed vs. variable width, 4-15
    Inserting, 4-13
    Selecting, 4-11
Communications management plans, 1-8
Connection methods, 7-10
Copyrights, 7-2
CS Live, 1-8
CSS styles
    Creating, 3-15
    Creating for link states, 5-14
    Creating, element, 3-20
    Inheritance, 3-21
    Overview of, 3-11
CSS Styles panel, 1-20, 3-15, 3-20

D

Definition lists, 3-6
Derivative works, 7-3
Div elements, 3-13
Document toolbar, 1-15
Document-relative links, 5-3
Documents
    Basic structure of, 2-22
    Zooming in and out on, 1-16
Download times, 7-5
Dynamic content, 2-9

E

Element styles, 3-13
    Creating, 3-20
E-mail links, 5-8
Extensible Hypertext Markup Language (XHTML), 1-2

F

Fair use, 7-3
Files
    Cloaking, 7-7
    Creating, 1-14
    Dependent, 7-14
    Getting from Web server, 7-14
    Guidelines for naming, 7-9
    Orphaned, 7-7
    Putting (uploading), 7-12
    Storing, 2-8
    Synchronizing, 7-14
Files panel, 1-15, 1-20, 7-12
Find and Replace, 2-31
Font sets, 3-20
Fonts, choosing, 1-11
FTP, 7-10

G

Getting files, 7-14
GIF format, 6-2

H

Heading levels, 3-2
Hexadecimal notation, 3-16
Home page, 1-2
Hotspots, 5-10
HTML, 1-2
    Tags, 2-22

Hyperlinks, 1-2

I

ID styles, 3-13
Image maps, 5-10
Images
    Attributes of, 6-5
    Background, 6-8
    File formats, 6-2
    Inserting, 1-30
Insert panel, 1-15
Intellectual property, 7-2
Interface, Dreamweaver, 1-14
Internet service providers (ISPs), 7-9
Internet, defined, 1-2

J

JPEG format, 6-2

L

Link states, 5-13
Links
    Checking, 7-7
    E-mail, 5-8
    External, 5-8
    Local, 5-3
    Named anchors, 5-5
    Setting targets of, 5-8
    Types of, 5-2
Lists
    Nested, 3-7
    Types of, 3-6
Local sites, 2-9

M

Model release, 7-3

N

Named anchors, 5-5
Nonbreaking spaces, 2-29

O

Ordered lists, 3-6
Orphaned files, 7-7

P

Page properties, 2-20
Page weight, 3-2, 7-5
Panel groups, 1-19
Panels, resizing, 1-20
PNG format, 6-3
Previewing Web pages, 1-32
Projects
    Lifecycle of, 1-5

    Reasons for failure of, 1-7
Property inspector, 1-15, 1-24, 3-21

Q

Quick Tag Editor, 2-24

R

RDS (Remote Data Services), 7-10
Related Files toolbar, 3-16
Root-relative links, 5-3
Rows
    Formatting, 4-11
    Inserting, 4-13
    Selecting, 4-11

S

Secure FTP, 7-10
Selectors, 3-13, 3-15
Special characters, inserting, 2-29
Spelling, checking, 7-5
Style sheets
    Creating external, 3-15
    External vs. internal, 3-12

T

Tables
    Borders, 4-18
    Fixed vs. variable width, 4-15
    Formatting, 4-10
    Inserting, 4-3
    Nested, 4-8
    Visual aids for, 4-4
    Writing summaries for, 4-5
Tag Editor, 2-23
Tag selector, 2-24
Text
    Alternate, 1-30, 5-10, 6-6
    Image-based, 6-4
    Inserting, 1-29, 2-17
    Selecting, 2-24
    Setting default color of, 2-20
    Setting size of, 3-20
Tiling, 6-8
Toolbars
    Coding, 2-23
    Document, 1-15
    Related Files, 3-16

U

Unordered lists, 3-6
URLs, 1-2

V

Visual aids, 1-16, 4-4
VSS (Visual SourceSafe), 7-10

W

Web pages
    Background colors, 2-20
    Creating, 2-15
    Design elements of, 1-11
    Linking to style sheet, 3-16
    Previewing, 1-32
    Typical elements of, 1-27
Web servers, 7-9
Web sites
    Local, 2-9

    Planning, 1-10, 2-2
    Uploading, 7-12
WebDAV, 7-10
Workspace Switcher, 1-19
Workspaces, creating custom, 1-19

X

XHTML, 1-2

Z

Zoom tools, 1-16